ISBN 978-0-942702-55-2

Published by:
Exchange Press, Inc.
17725 NE 65th Street, B-275
Redmond, WA 98052
(800) 221-2864
www.ChildCareExchange.com

Cover Design: Scott Bilstad

The joy of this book is the narratives that frame the thinking; the moments and journeys that connect us all in a larger story that we don't yet know. Ann and Dylan's explorations of the natural world braid together to create a map of pathways, stillness, and joy to create a map that in itself demonstrates a reverence of nature; there is a true connection to each other that allows them both to share their awakening thoughts (or developing souls) without pressure. A gentle and thought-provoking book.

Claire Warden, Mindstretchers Ltd.

This book, certain to become an instant classic, recounts two parallel journeys through the world of nature around us. I am not sure whose discoveries—toddler's or adult's—absorbed and moved me more. I also appreciated the scholarly notes on pedagogical principles, theoretical sources, and word etymologies interspersed gently, sliding among the diary entries that carry their own resonance and literary power. Ann Pelo is a master teacher and writer, and this book enriches and honors the field of early childhood.

Carolyn Edwards, editor, *The Hundred Languages of Children: The Reggio Emilia Experience in Transformation* (1993); *The Hundred Languages of Children: The Reggio Emilia Approach to Early Childhood Education* (2012)

Thank you for this wonderful book! Ann's language is lyrical, and her pedagogy is inspiring. Her book will have a profound effect on my practice as both a preschool teacher, and a pedagogical specialist. Her gentle and poignant insights have already changed how see I my own children and their growing ecological identities!

Megan Arnim, Teacher, Hilltop Children's Center, Seattle, Washington

The story Ann tells so beautifully in *The Goodness of Rain* will touch your heart, your mind, and your soul. You'll feel something shifting within you as you read this book, and you'll begin to see rain and the rest of the natural world in a whole new way. The impact of the book is profound and something that will stay with you long after you read the last page.

Ruth Wilson, author of *Nature and Young Children*, Second Edition (2012)

the
Goodness
of Rain

Developing an Ecological Identity in Young Children

by Ann Pelo

For Dylan

I will show you the trail
and this is what it will lead you to:

a thousand friendships that will offer
honey in little thorny cups,
the secrets of the underbrush,
the health of sunlight,
suppleness of body,

the unafraidness of the night,
the delight of deep water,
the goodness of rain,
the story of the trail,
the knowledge of wetlands,
the aloofness of knowing.

Ernest Thompson Seton, *Woodland Tales*

Ernest Thompson Seton, *Woodland Tales*.
Santa Fe, NM: Seton Village Press, 1940.

Table of Contents

Gratitude 24

Foreword 26

Introduction — A Year Outside, Together
  Developing an Ecological Self 29

Finding Place
  Ecological Literacy as Our Way Home 39

Walk the Land 55

  Triptych: Apple Knowledge
  Footsteps on the Ground

Practice Silence 73

  Eagles and Salmon
  Reverence

Learn the Names 93

  Bird Year
  Naming and Knowing

Embrace Sensuality 111

First Snow
Full-bodied Participation

Explore New Perspectives 127

Life and Death
Seeing with New Eyes

Create Stories 151

Eat Like Heron
Telling a Good Story

Make Rituals 165

Pooh Sticks
Gestures of Hope and Gratitude

A Call to Come Home 179

Coda
    One Wild Spirit 187

Gratitude

"I will show you the trail and this is what it will lead you to: a thousand friendships that will offer honey. . . ." Honey, yes, offered by good and generous companions, sustaining me while this book took shape.

During my year with Dylan I'd often call my dear friends Susan Alexander and Margie Carter, eager to share a tender, or funny, or astonishing story about an experience I'd had with Dylan. They delighted and marveled with me, and encouraged me to write down my stories.

And so I wrote. And I shared that first writing with people who I counted on both to celebrate it and to challenge me to take the writing and the thinking to new places. Gratitude to those first readers: Bill Bigelow carried my ideas into his days with his grandson, a sort of 'field testing' that affirmed that the book held resonance beyond memoir; a fellow writer, he reminded me of the value of precision and clarity in writing, alongside the drunken lyricism to which I am susceptible. Tenneson Woolf called out the ideas in the book as practices for a way of being in the world, moving the book from an educator's effort toward principles for teaching to the terrain of spirit and heart. My parents, Carol and Ken Pelo, exclaimed with pride just as they did when I brought home my first scrawled sentences in kindergarten; their pride swelled under me like a wave. Dylan's parents, Alexis Squier and Jack Grey, held me true to Dylan and to the joy of our year together. Susan and Margie urged me to keep writing.

I'd written other books and plenty of journal articles before this book, as an educator writing to other educators about teaching and learning. *The Goodness of Rain* is a different sort of book, and required me to find a new voice as a writer. Gratitude to the writers, teachers, and students with whom I studied and experimented and made false starts and found my way: fellow participants during a sunny May week at the Environmental Writing Institute at the University of Montana; writers at the Thunder Arm Writing Retreat at the North Cascades Institute; the crew at Orion's 2011 Wildbranch Writing Workshop.

I found just the right home for this book and for me—Exchange Press. Editor Bonnie Neugebauer held the book's intention and spirit with generous and gentle care. Production editor Carole White stewarded the book to publication, cheerfully engaging the details while tending carefully to the integrity of the book's character. Design editor Scott Bilstad crafted a visual expression of the soul of the book; I wept when I first saw his design, feeling how truly he understood the book, and my hopes for it.

Eli Sterling has been companion throughout. He was at my side during the full-hearted close of my year with Dylan, and cheered me on in my move to the country to explore the notion of ecological identity through daily life in a cabin in the woods. He celebrated the book's evolution, listening by the fire in the evening as I read the day's writing. He thought with me about ideas at the heart of the book: the meaning of ritual, the role of stories, the necessary gestures of reverence. And as I worked to finish the book, Eli worked to finish construction on a house for us to come home to. In that home together, the honey flows sweet indeed. Gratitude. Gratitude. Gratitude.

Foreword by Robert Michael Pyle

The notion of the mentor molding the young charge, like clay
in the hands of a master potter, is an old one. What is less often
remarked, even forgotten, is that the molding goes both ways.
This is what I especially came away with from this richly affirming
book: that the show & tell of the big wide world is a two-way deal.

What an awesome thing! To have the everyday company of a year-
old person, and the responsibility for how her next year is largely
spent. When Ann Pelo becomes Dylan's daily minder, she deter-
mines that, as much as possible, those days will be spent out-of-
doors. No nature deficit for this child. If every nanny (or mommy
or dad or day-care leader) adopted such an itinerary—lake and
duck to crow and rhodie, apple to bug to slug, garden to park to
bramble patch—there would be no last child in the woods.

A laudable plan for sure, to get the kid out. But how to go about it?
"What are the earliest offerings we can make in a child's life?"
Ann asks. "How do we find the surprise waiting in the details that
we know so well? These questions shaped my days with Dylan."
And what did those days contain?

"The slow gold closing of a California poppy at dusk . . . our
footprints on the land . . . its mist and dust and scent." A tiny
fish in hand, "its flash and spark, its dart and dapple . . . the great
cavalcading world of crows and blackberry brambles and worms on
the sidewalk." Everything, in fact, that "the world offers us today."

Ann's companion "pulled off her clothes, went barefoot, picked up
stones and leaves and twigs, jumped into mud, dipped her fingers
into rainwater runoff . . . all senses on call." Little things, yet shared
revelations that bring up large lessons: "When we turn toward the
Earth with curiosity and sympathy, with humility and wonder, our
lives fall into place—we fall into place."

A writer of uncommon elegance and grace, Ann Pelo charts her days outside with Dylan. In between these small adventures (or large, for a small person), she shares what she has come to know about falling into place, and how we should act when we get there. *The Goodness of Rain*'s clear stream of prose is equally illumined by the field trip reports and the author's meditations. But just as much, I enjoyed the conversations—with a baby? Yes! Ann explains a butterfly's death, and Dylan responds: "Butterfly hurt wing. All done!" As they say, out of the mouths of babes . . . it *is* conversation!

Because Ann declines to lecture, Dylan makes her own discoveries—and through them, she teaches Ann as well. This is where the two-way street comes in. "I learned from Dylan the meaning of the oft-spoken adage that we ought to look at the world the way a child looks, 'as if for the first time,' and, so, I slowed down—way, way down. Lifting a raindrop from her coat sleeve and balancing it on her tongue . . . Dylan demonstrated how to participate physically and heartily in the world."

In this pure and wonderful book, Ann Pelo shares such vital knowledge with us. I do not know and cannot imagine a better or lovelier argument for taking our children OUT—and letting them take us too—from a very early age. *The Goodness of Rain* discovers not only its title message, in a rainy city where it is a good thing to know and believe; but also the goodness of life, and living, and paying attention, even as a small child does.

Robert Michael Pyle is a naturalist and a Guggenheim Fellow residing along a tributary of the Lower Columbia. His 17 books include the John Burroughs Medal-winning Wintergreen *and* Mariposa Road. *Considered a classic in the literature of children and nature, Pyle's book* The Thunder Tree *has recently been re-issued by Oregon State University Press. He loves to take his grandchildren out-of-doors.*

A Year Outside, Together

Developing an Ecological Self

*I believe we live in the body of the world
and that we are compelled to know the world.
We are compelled to witness.*

Sharman Apt Russell, *Standing in the Light*

Sharman Apt Russell, *Standing in the Light: My Life as a Pantheist*.
New York: Basic Books, 2008.

Eighteen-month-old Dylan stands at the back door of her house, looking out at the yard edged with the garden's green rows and overhung with a deep purple plum tree. As I finish preparing our lunch, I ask Dylan where she'd like to eat it. Dylan answers, simply, "Outside." And so we spread a picnic blanket on the backyard lawn and eat our lunch under the sky.

An hour later, we carry our plates and the picnic blanket inside; it's time for Dylan's nap. When I reach to close the back door, Dylan cries out, "No! No close doors! Open, please!"

Yes! Doors open, and the whole living world waiting outside, beckoning to us.

I was Dylan's caregiver for a year, from her first birthday to her second. My commitment during that year was that we would spend each day outside, no matter the weather, experiencing the land and sky through the nuances of each unfolding season. I hoped that our days outside would make us intimates of the patch of the earth where Dylan and her family lived: a suburban Seattle neighborhood built on a hill and overlooking a lake. The hill is nameless; the neighborhood built onto it is known as View Ridge, named for its eastward vista across Lake Washington to the Cascade Mountains. This terrain is where Dylan and I spent our days, exploring what lies around the hill, what grows there and who lives there and how the sky arcs over it. A bike trail curves along the bottom of the hill, making a green tunnel of maple and cedar, fern and blackberry. A former Navy airfield stands as a 350-acre park on the shores of the lake at the foot of the hill, with beaches tucked alongside tall grass meadows and blackberry thickets, and trails through wetlands, and an old orchard. North of the hill and west of it, two creeks meander through backyards and greenswards. And in the neighborhood built onto the hill, the sidewalks have cracks where weeds grow, and telephone wires where birds perch, and the houses have yards with grass and flowers and trees, some untended and some carefully manicured.

Each morning, Dylan and I walked her sister to kindergarten at the public elementary school six blocks from their home. Then we set out on our own, walking or biking or taking the bus to some living and lively green place.

In each season, there were gray days and bright ones. The air was sometimes mild, sometimes damp and cool, sometimes shivery. In each season, there was rain: rain that misted and sputtered, spit and sprinkled and torrented, leaving its imprint on the land in puddles and wet soil and squelching grass, in raindrops shimmering on leaves and hung as crystals along bare branches. Rain defined this landscape as surely as the hill, the lake, the mountains on the horizon.

In each season, every day, no matter the weather, Dylan and I went outside.

My commitment was to both of us. I hoped that Dylan would learn the place where she lived, would take it into her bones and blood so that it would become bound into her identity. I hoped that I would relax my shoulders that hunched against the rain, and open my resistant heart to this place where I make my home at a far remove from the sage scrub and pine lands that are bound into my body as home terrain. I hoped that our days outside would cultivate in each of us an ecological identity.

Before my year with Dylan, I'd spent two decades in Seattle as an early childhood educator. For most of that time, I worked as a teacher in a full-day child care program, with three-, four-, and five-year-old children. Over time, I gradually folded teacher education into my work, and eventually that became my primary focus. I cared deeply about social justice teaching and learning, and about how to use the languages of art for inquiry, for critical thinking, and for collaborative creating. At the heart of my work with children and with teachers was the conviction that learning happens in relationship, and that it is most resonant when it grows from authentic exchange and responsive engagement with ideas and experiences that matter.

That was my professional life.

Around that life—which was rich and consuming—I spent as much time outside as I could. I was happiest out-of-doors, consciously and dizzyingly happy, and I sought out such fierce happiness anywhere I could find it. I kept a backyard garden at the apartment building where I lived, and slept on the building's rooftop deck on summer nights. I strapped on boots to hike in the Cascade Mountains on weekends, and traveled several times a year to the red rock desert of southeast Utah for week-long solo backpacking trips. I rode my bike to work, I volunteered on a farm outside Seattle, I met friends for walks instead of coffee.

These threads—education and the outdoors—were on separate spindles for many years. When I began to weave them together as warp and weft, I discovered a new pattern for my life.

In 2005, I traveled to Australia for my work, and met Janet Robertson, an early childhood educator at Mia Mia, the Child and

Family Centre at the Institute of Early Childhood in Sydney. She'd just returned from an internship in Scandinavia to study the forest kindergartens there, and was keen to share her experiences. As I listened to her enthusiastic stories and watched her translate what she'd learned into daily practice at Mia Mia, I felt the ground re-aligning into a new terrain. A forest kindergarten is, most simply put, preschool, outdoors, all day. This compelled me! Children and adults outside, paying attention to the world that holds us, delighting in it, wondering about it, making meaning of it together—this dazzled my heart, left me tearful and exultant. I felt both yearning and the end of yearning.

I returned home and began to read about the history of forest kindergartens and their current manifestations around the world, about eco-literacy and place-based education. I lingered with the writing of David Orr, Claire Warden, Richard Louv, David Sobel. And I began to integrate what I read into my teaching and my writing, considering how to craft a pedagogy for ecology at the school where I worked.

Around that same time, I began to consider moving away from Seattle. I didn't feel easy in the damp and gray Northwest, though I'd accustomed myself to its moody climate and closed-in geography, all mountains and trees overarching and ferns underfoot. I longed for the pine trees and open sky of my childhood in Eastern Washington, for dusty heat in summer and for sun-shimmered snow in winter. The liveliness that I felt in that land lay dormant during my years in Seattle, no matter how much time I spent outside.

I wanted to find my way home—not literally back to my childhood terrain, but to "living where landscape is part of your life" (Amy

Irvine), embraced and embracing. I wanted to slide past urban buffers into skin-to-skin intimacy with land that I loved.

Where to live? How to make a life? Questions of place were always whispering at me. Should I abandon the Northwest for Utah's elemental red rock or Montana's Big Sky? Should I take up new work to express and feed the intimacy I wanted with the earth—start a forest kindergarten or become an environmental educator? Or should I leave education altogether, and become a national park ranger or a farmer?

To open space and time for these questions, I decided to step away from teaching for a year, leaving my school and entering a year of listening to what was calling to me, a discernment year. How should I spend that year? What would help me listen?

I considered taking graduate classes in environmental humanities and place-based education. I imagined myself reading hungrily, talking late into the night with fellow students, writing my way to clarity of purpose, writing my way home.

Instead, I spent a year with a baby, a year outside, together. A dear baby of a dear friend, a baby I'd known since she was born; Dylan's child care was in flux at the same time that I was considering how to shape my discernment year. Dylan's mama invited me to be Dylan's caregiver for a year; my startled delight at her invitation illuminated my course: I would spend my listening year with Dylan. My questions about place and home, about work and the world beyond walls were bound into that year.

This book describes the way that I lived into those questions during my days with Dylan.

I set out with the intention of nurturing Dylan's ecological identity, wanting her life to be well-rooted in place—wanting her to be at home in her native land, as I remembered being as a child, as I was not as an adult. I imagined that the year would hold riches for Dylan, in her ecological development. I hadn't imagined that it would hold such significance for my ecological development.

In 1965—the year I was born—Supreme Court Justice William O. Douglas proposed that the United States adopt a Wilderness Bill of Rights. He published his proposal as part of a manifesto on the necessity of wilderness in our lives as humans. Here are elements of his Wilderness Bill of Rights:

> *We believe in the right of children to an understanding of their place in nature's community, of which they are a part.*
>
> *We believe in their right to acquire skills for living in the out-of-doors as part of their heritage, to swim, to fish, to manage a canoe, to climb, to hike.*
>
> *We believe in their right of discovery and adventure in nature's world.*
>
> *We believe in their right to friendly comradeship with someone older, likewise an adventurer in the out-of-doors.*
>
> *We believe in their need of the healing found in the wilderness of nature.*
>
> *We believe in their unfolding response to the warm earth, the friendly stars, the music of streams, the unknown life in the hidden places, great trees, sunsets, and storms.*

This articulation of what it is to root ourselves in 'nature's community' captures the spirit with which I set out on my year with Dylan; these were the rights I wanted to offer her. During that year outside with Dylan, I learned that when we engage these rights for children, we live into them ourselves.

References

William O. Douglas, *A Wilderness Bill of Rights*.
Boston: Little, Brown, and Company, 1965.

Amy Irvine, *Trespass: Living at the Edge of the Promised Land*.
New York: North Point Press, 2008.

Sharman Apt Russell, *Standing in the Light: My Life as a Pantheist*.
New York: Basic Books, 2008.

Finding Place

Ecological Literacy as
Our Way Home

To climb these coming crests
one word to you,
to you and your children:
stay together
learn the flowers
go light.

Gary Snyder, "For the Children"

Dylan and I stand face-to-face with a sunflower. Dylan is in her baby carrier strapped to my chest, and the sunflower is at her eye level. The flower blooms in bold yellow perfection. Moving purposefully across the flower's dark center, a bee gathers pollen. We watch, Dylan and I, as the bee burrows into the bristle-stiff stamens, dusts its belly with pollen and, then, with quick flicks, transfers the yellow dust from its body into the pouches on its back legs. The bee's movements are elegant and compelling, and Dylan and I watch long and in silence as it flies from one tiny patch of the sunflower's center to another, burrowing, then combing the pollen from its belly. There is, for us, only this sunflower and this bee; the world is contained in this moment, and all of life is manifest in the dance of the bee's legs. We are in no hurry, Dylan and I; there is nothing better for us to do than to watch this bee in this sunflower.

Every day, we walk past the garden where this sunflower grows. It's on the route we take home after we walk Dylan's sister to school. Every day, we pause at this garden to notice what's growing and what's dying, what's just emerging from the ground and what's gone. Through the fall, the petals of the sunflower will curl and brown and dry and drop, and its face will tilt forward, and its stem will buckle under that shifted weight, and one day, it will be gone. As fall unfolds into winter, we'll play with the raindrops that collect on the plum-purple leaves of the smokebush. In early spring, the daphnes' perfume will bend us low to breathe its sweet scent. Daffodils will appear overnight and grow inches every day until they open in yellow trumpets. And, so, through the year, the garden will tell its stories of the seasons, until it returns to the first story we heard there, the story of the sunflower, as Dylan and I come full-circle to another August, where our year together began.

We are born ready to befriend sunflowers.

Animals alongside other animals, we are born with a keen awareness of the buzzing, breezing, shining, misting, singing, and silent life that flows across this Earth. Attuned to shadow and light, to movement both predictable and unexpected, to the dip and rise of temperature, to the varying cries of earthbound and sky-chased creatures, we are born into the wide, wild Earth, and our first instinct is to know it.

This instinct too quickly becomes buried beneath the rip-rap of contemporary life: beneath plastic toys and alphabet drills, beneath homework and housework and blue-glowing screens, beneath numbing commutes and smart phones and long days at work. But the instinct to know the Earth as animals know their home grounds is essential to a full human life, and must be safeguarded as birthright in young children, and retrieved, rekindled, and renewed in us adults.

We teach children to write and to read and to navigate mathematical systems so that they can access the world of ideas and questions and intellectual exchange. We teach children how to behave with other people so that they can grow joyful and nourishing relationships. We teach children history, so that they know where they come from, and we teach them art, so that they can imagine what might be, and we teach them science so that they understand the intricate workings of the physical world. This teaching honors and strengthens children's innate social, intellectual, cultural, and aesthetic identities, identities that we value as a society. We don't leave their development to happenstance or luck. Just so, we must nurture children's intrinsic ecological identities with intentional and attentive action.

This is our work as parents, caregivers, teachers: to invite children to braid their identities together with the place where they live by calling their attention to the air, the sky, the cracks in the sidewalk where the earth bursts out of its cement cage.

When we live this way with children, we align ourselves with the instinct to know the place where we live. Inviting children to know their home ground is our way home, as well.

Knowledge of the House

The Australian eco-philosopher, Val Plumwood, proposes two tasks for us as citizens. The first task is to re-situate the human within the ecological, and the second is to re-situate the beyond-human within the ethical. These two tasks, taken together, instruct us about the foundational elements in the development of an ecological identity. First, find place. Then, set a moral compass that takes its bearings from humble and caring consideration of that place, and of all places. Our work as teachers and parents encompasses these two tasks, as we strive to strengthen in children—and in ourselves—an ecological identity.

"The word *ecology* means literally 'knowledge of the house'," writes Jack Collom. "In the sense that our house is now the entire world, the study of ecology has come to be a comprehensive study of the relational."

To nurture ecological identity in young children, we invite them into relationship with the world beyond walls and with the creatures that live there. We invite them into ethical thinking anchored by the compassion that comes from caring and engaged relationships. We invite them to come home to the Earth, and to live honorably in that home.

During my year with Dylan, 'home' meant the fragrance of just-fallen cedar boughs and the heady scent of gasoline at the lake; it meant the tart sweetness of blackberries and the scratch of blackberry thorns, the light gray of near-constant clouds, the tread of the cracks and curves of the sidewalks near Dylan's home. It was a gladness to offer Dylan this as her home ground.

Other places are less compelling as home ground. What does it mean to nurture an ecological identity when the immediate environment numbs rather than delights the senses? What can be embraced in a neighborhood dominated by concrete, cars, and convenience stores?

There is wide-ranging inequality in children's opportunities to meet the Earth's humming life, a disparity that is token of and testament to the unjust organization of our society. That unevenness of opportunity demands bold community action aimed at remedying the inequity of environmental racism and classism.

Every child deserves to know the pulsing, cycling life of the Earth through simple intimacies and daily encounters. Every child deserves a world beyond walls in which they know, as Barry Lopez writes, "where on this Earth one goes, what one touches, the patterns one observes in nature—the intricate history of one's life in the land, even a life in the city, where wind, the chirp of birds, the line of a falling leaf, are known."

Children's worlds are small, detailed places—the crack in the sidewalk receives their full attention, as does the earthworm flipping over and over on the pavement after rainfall. Children give themselves over to a place: they poke sticks into slivers of dirt in the pavement, they float leaves in the curbside run-off, they dig holes in the flowerboxes that flank a shop doorway. They have access to elements of the natural world that many adults don't acknowledge. When we, like children, tune ourselves more finely, we find the natural world waiting for us: the daily and seasonal cycles of light and dark, the feel and scent of the air, the particularities of the sky—these are elements of the natural world and can begin to anchor us in a place. "Wherever you are and whatever your resources," writes Rachel Carson in *The Sense of Wonder*, "You can look up at the sky—its dawn and twilight beauties, its moving clouds, its stars by night. You can listen to the wind. . . . You can feel the rain on your face and think of its long journey, its many transmutations, from sea to air to earth."

Rather than contribute to a sense of disconnection from place by writing off our most urban environments as unsalvageable or not worth knowing, we can instill in children an attitude of attention to what exists of the natural world in their neighborhoods. The sense of care for and connection to place, then, can become the foundation for critical examination of how that place has been degraded, as children grow older. Rick Bass, in *The Book of Yaak*, describes his experience of the interplay between love of place and willingness to see the human damage done to that place: "As it became my home, the wounds that were being inflicted upon it—the insults—became my own."

Every child lives someplace. And that someplace begins to matter when children are invited to know where they are and to participate in the unfolding life of that place—coming to know the changes in the light and in the feel of the air, and participating in a community of people who speak of such things to each other.

Listen! Look! Linger long enough that your shadow lengthens and your heart contracts with the knife-edged sharpness that signals the arrival of a new love. Move through the world differently—tenderly, fiercely, modestly—aligning yourself with the lay of the land, with the reach of the sky, with the movement of the water. Say "we" when you speak of the Earth, and take the Earth with you to the voting booth, to public meetings and zoning hearings, to family reunions and school potlucks. Learn the names of the birds that pass through your backyard, of the insects that fly through your windows, of the clouds that shape-change in the sky above your street. Learn the names, and speak them, and teach them to your neighbors.

This is what it means to grow an ecological identity.

The Disposition to Delight

Ecological identity is bound together with ecological literacy, which is, at its core, whole-hearted delight in and curiosity about and knowledge of the beyond-human world. Ecological literacy is anchored by core dispositions, habits of mind and heart that play out over time to become a person's essential ecological nature.

Dylan at the sunflower offers an example of the dispositions at the heart of ecological literacy.

Pay attention. Look closely and for long stretches of time. Look often enough that you notice change and constancy. Notice details. Notice context. Notice rhythm, texture, pattern.

Be curious. Look for connections. Look for novelty. Wonder at the connections and at the novelty. Consider the details: What purpose might they serve in the life of the thing you're observing?

Open your heart. Be astonished and delighted. Marvel! Feel gratitude. Grieve. With all the empathy in you, embrace the life of the thing before you.

Be modest and humble. Move from recognition of your rightful place in the world, which is neither distinct from nor superior to nor less natural than the other beings, the rocks, the dirt, the growing things and the decaying things with whom we share the planet.

"Wherever you turn your eyes, the world can shine like transfiguration," writes Marilynne Robinson, in *Gilead*. "You don't have to bring a thing to it except a little willingness to see. Only, who could have the courage to see it?" Such courage is the animating spirit of an ecological identity.

The disposition to see, with an open heart and curious mind and humble spirit, both reflects and sustains a particular way of understanding one's relationship to the natural world and one's role in it. When we strengthen in children the disposition to participate fully in the majesty and the delicacy of the natural world, we strengthen such a capacity in ourselves, and we learn alongside children how to be ecologically literate.

How do we cultivate the courage to see, the disposition to participate? What are the daily practices that develop ecological literacy? What are the earliest offerings we can make in a child's life? I worried at these questions during my year with Dylan, wondering when to teach and when to be silent, mulling over the places we ought to visit to experience the intimacy of familiarity and the places we ought to visit to experience the new awareness that comes with novelty.

Tentatively, deliberately, I felt my way into a pedagogy of looking and listening. I grew a handful of daily practices by which I charted my days with Dylan: *walk the land; practice silence; learn the names: embrace sensuality; explore new perspectives; create stories; make rituals.* These practices are integrated ways of behaving in the world. None is sufficient in itself; each is useful, but incomplete. When taken together, though, in all their contradictory and complementary qualities, they can become a pedagogy for ecological literacy.

The Instinct for Experience

This pedagogy takes some effort, some attention. We have to go out of our way—we have to take children out of their way—to engage the wide, wild world that exists beyond classroom walls and computer screens.

Biologist and natural history educator Robert Michael Pyle writes eloquently of 'the extinction of experience' with wild places and wildlife, which is, he declares, as devastating for the natural world as the extinction of species:

"Direct, personal contact with other living things affects us in vital ways that vicarious experience can never replace. . . . A face-to-face encounter with a banana slug means much more than a Komodo dragon seen on television. . . . One of the greatest causes of the ecological crisis is the state of personal alienation from nature in which many people live. We lack a widespread sense of intimacy with the living world."

Pyle goes on to ask, famously and poignantly, "What is the extinction of the condor to a child who has never known a wren?"

His question propels us out the door and beyond the walls into the world of wrens and robins, worms on the sidewalk and wind that scatters leaves along the street, banana slugs and beetles — out the door and into the world of experience, because experience matters.

Walk the land, both silently and exclaiming. Learn the names of what we encounter there, even as we linger in sensuality and delight. Tell stories and make rituals about what we experience in the world beyond walls. Invite children to weave that green and growing world into their hearts. And in all this, work with the same tender and fierce protectiveness against the extinction of experience as we work against the extinction of leatherback sea turtles and Siberian tigers.

We live in a culture that dismisses the significance of an ecological identity, a culture that posits that we make home by the simple fact of habitation, rather than by intimate connection to the land, the sky, the air. Any place can become home, we're told. Which means, really, that no place is home.

This is a dangerous view. When no place is home, a dammed river is regrettable, but not a devastating blow to the heart. When no place is home, eating food grown thousands of miles away is normal, and the cost to the planet of processing and shipping it is easy to ignore. When no place is home, roads bulldozed into wilderness for logging and mining make us wince—and look away. When no place is home, the daily extinction of a hundred species is an abstract loss, a number to exclaim at, but not a compelling grief that propels us to the statehouse and to corporate boardrooms.

An ecological identity offers an antidote to the displacement that makes possible the wounding and wrecking of the planet. When we turn toward the Earth with curiosity and sympathy, with humility and wonder, our lives fall into place—we fall into place. The earth, the sky, the water, and their beyond-human beings have our attention, and we begin to behave toward them with propriety. We take the Earth into account in our personal decisions and we demand that government and industry take the Earth into account, as well. Cultivating in ourselves and in our children an ecological identity becomes a conscious act of rebellion against the displacement of our times and the ruinous consequences of that displacement.

The Moral Power of Wonder

Now, especially, when life on Earth is in jeopardy, ecological identity is essential. Delight and astonishment, curiosity and exploration—these surely blossom into love and knowledge. And love and knowledge propel right action, which is what this

Earth needs from us. Whether we are, at this juncture, simply bearing witness to the death of the planet or somehow, implausibly and miraculously, holding that death at bay, it is essential to our integrity that we act in faithful allegiance to the Earth.

Kathleen Dean Moore, ethical philosopher, speaks of "the moral power of wonder." "Radical amazement," she writes, "leads to radical compassion." And radical compassion spills over into moral behavior and concerted action in defense of the beyond-human world.

Moore elaborates on the ethical repercussions of wonder, of compassion, of love:

To love—a person and a place—means at least this:
  1. *To want to be near it, physically.*
  2. *To want to know everything about it—its story, its moods, what it looks like by moonlight.*
  3. *To rejoice in the fact of it.*
  4. *To fear its loss, and grieve for its injuries.*
  5. *To protect it—fiercely, mindlessly, futilely, and maybe tragically, but to be helpless to do otherwise.*
  6. *To be transformed in its presence—lifted, lighter on your feet, transparent, open to everything beautiful and new.*
  7. *To want to be joined with it, taken in by it, lost in it.*
  8. *To want the best for it.*
  9. *Desperately.*
  10. *To love a person or a place is to take responsibility for its well-being.*

I think again of Plumwood's two tasks: locate ourselves in the beyond-human world, and develop an ethic that holds us accountable to that lively and living world. These tasks, done well, spill us into a renewed moral relationship with the Earth, love made tangible by our right behavior. Integrated into place, we act on behalf of place. The Earth's land and sky and creatures become protagonists in our moral understandings and deliberations.

Moore concludes her list of the implications of love with a declaration that serves as instruction for living from an ecological identity: "Obligation grows from love. Love isn't just a state of being, it's a way of acting in the world. Love isn't a sort of bliss, it's a kind of work. It is the natural shape of caring."

References

Rick Bass, *The Book of Yaak*.
Boston: Houghton Mifflin Company, 1996.

Rachel Carson, *The Sense of Wonder*.
New York: HarperCollins, 1965.

Jack Collom, "An Ecosystem of Writing Ideas."
Exquisite Corpse: A Journal of Letters and Life,
Issue 9, Summer 2001.

Barry Lopez, "Landscape and Narrative." In *Crossing Open Ground*.
New York: Scribners, 1988.

Kathleen Dean Moore, *The Pine Island Paradox:
Making Connections in a Disconnected World*.
Minneapolis: Milkweed Editions, 2004.

David Orr, *Ecological Literacy:
Education and the Transition to a Postmodern World*.
Albany: State University of New York Press, 1992.

Val Plumwood, cited by Deborah Bird Rose at
http://ecologicalhumanities.org/rose.html.

Robert Michael Pyle, *The Thunder Tree:
Lessons from an Urban Wildland*.
New York: Houghton Mifflin, 1993.

Marilynne Robinson, *Gilead*.
New York: Farrar, Straus, and Giroux, 2004.

Gary Snyder, "For the Children." In *No Nature: New and Selected
Poems*. New York: Pantheon Books, 1992.

Walk the Land

Triptych: Apple Knowledge

On our way to the beach on a bright September morning, Dylan and I stop at the children's garden in Magnuson Park. The sunflowers there are in their full glory, and it seems a shame to hurry past them to get to the beach. I take Dylan's hand and walk with her into the sunflower grove, and what beauty they are! They reach over our heads; their thick green stems are like saplings and the yellow undersides of their faces glow with the sun shining through them.

At the far end of the sunflower patch, we find a trail that curves up a spiraled hill. The incline, and the path's gravel, make the climb up the hill an effort for Dylan, who, at fifteen months old, has just begun to walk. But I want Dylan to be able to look down at the sunflowers that overarched us when we stood below them, so I encourage her up the path to the top.

And the perspective down onto the upturned rounds of the sunflowers is worth the climb. Tall stems hidden by bold faces, the flowers offer themselves like floating lanterns, emanating light in the sun's bright glow. We admire the sunflowers, Dylan and I, and then turn to take in the rest of the vista from our hilltop perch. And a surprise reveals itself: a small apple orchard tucked against the spiral hill below us, invisible from the children's garden where we've just been.

The orchard becomes our destination.

I carry Dylan down the spiral path to the orchard and set her at its edge. There are a half-dozen rows of squat trees, limbs splayed onto supporting wire to form low apple hedges. Heirloom trees, their evocative names have been inked onto metal tags on their trunks: Liberty, Prairie Spy, Macoun. The deep reds and blushing pinks catch Dylan's attention: "Appa!" she calls out in startled recognition: familiar fruit in an unfamiliar context. She tucks herself under a low-limbed tree whose boughs are heavy with satin-red apples, and I step back to watch.

The light, sweet breath of apples scents the air, and the warm autumn sun makes for easy lingering. Dylan reaches into the tree, flips a leaf, and laughs. Another leaf, another flip, more laughter. Her hand moves from leaf to branch, and she runs her fingers along the ridges and roughs of the bark. The branch leads her to an apple. She touches her fingertips to its red curve, then cups the apple in her hand, tightens her fingers around it, and, leaning close, bites into the apple as it hangs from the branch. Mouth full of juice and autumn's flesh, she grins at me. "Appa," she says, a confirmation.

With a few more bites and their accompanying tugs, the apple drops into Dylan's lap. She picks it up, lifts it toward me. I take a bite, marveling at the apple's sweet fragrance, and at its sharp, tart tang, and at Dylan's taste for it. I return the apple to Dylan. She takes a few more bites, then drops the apple, letting it lie among the windfall under the tree.

The ancient story: an apple plucked from a tree by an innocent, awakening knowledge. But not a fall *from* grace, here in the apple orchard: instead, a fall *into* grace. Into the knowledge of apple in its right context, not mounded in the grocery store or tucked into a basket on the kitchen counter or sliced into manageable toddler-sized crescents for lunch. Apple where it was born, where it grew from bud to blossom to fruit. Apple on a rough-barked limb, tucked among leaves that shimmer in the autumn sun. Falling into the grace of apple knowledge.

Just up the street from Dylan's home, an apple tree grows in a neighbor's yard. We pass it each day as we come and go, and often we stop to look close, to touch the apples, to admire their curves and breathe in the scent, which tells the story of autumn.

"Appa! Appa!" Dylan calls as we approach the tree, even when it's several houses away and out of sight around a curve in the road. She knows that the apple tree is ahead; nestled in a baby sling against my chest, she shimmies her shoulders, claps her hands, looks into my eyes with an eager grin. When we finally encounter the tree, her delight bubbles into laughter and more cries of "Appa! Appa!" Dylan greets the tree like a beloved friend encountered after a too-long absence.

The autumn weeks pass, and the apples begin to fall to the ground unharvested. I ask in the neighborhood about the house and learn that it's for sale, and that the owners are not in residence; a caretaker comes every few weeks to tend to the house and yard. Hearing this, I rejoice.

The next time that Dylan and I pass the tree, I lift Dylan out of the sling and hold her high among the branches. "Dylan," I say. "We can eat these apples." Dylan doesn't look at me, but gazes at the apples hanging around her. I'm quiet, she's quiet. She reaches for the nearest apple and tugs—and then she's holding the apple, and grinning at me. I take a bite, opening the apple's flesh for Dylan, who claims it, then, with her own lusty bite. Chewing, she turns to look at me, juice dribbling onto her chin. "Appa," she declares, then returns to eating.

After this ceremonial first harvest, we pick an apple each time we pass.

September becomes October, and October melts into November. The autumn sunlight pales, the air takes on a cold edge, rain becomes a frequent companion. The leaves turn red-brown and fall from the apple tree; Dylan adds 'leaf' to her vocabulary.

One day, we pick the last apple. "All done," Dylan says. "All done." This becomes her winter refrain, passing the bare limbs of the apple tree. "Appa all done."

The weeks pass; winter's rain carries us through the dark months and floats us into March. Dylan and I pass our neighborhood apple tree in our damp comings and goings, stopping there sometimes to lift beaded raindrops from the rough branches onto our fingertips, winter's fruit where apples once grew. "Apples all done," Dylan says each time we pass the tree, a ritual acknowledgment of absence.

As spring shoulders through the rain, finally outpacing winter, buds take shape along the tree's bare limbs, the tiniest of bumps, noticeable more by touch than by gaze. I point them out to Dylan, who dutifully runs her fingers along the branches and repeats my naming: "Buds," she says, a static word, not part of a story that compels her, certainly not part of the story that she knows about this tree, the story of apples pulled from branches, apples that drip juice and awaken tongue.

Then one day, we pass the tree and it's as though the branches have been silked in green overnight. No longer brown branches with little knobby bumps, but awash in green: delicate, tiny leaves are layered over the bark. And only a few days later, the palest of pinks joins the fresh bright green: blossoms, a froth, a foam, a drama. Blossoms, a delight in their own right. But still not part of the story of apples, not yet, not for Dylan.

Soon after the apple blossoms appear, I take Dylan to a parkland full of cherry trees—the quad at the University of Washington, ringed in trees—twenty? thirty? more? They fill the formal green mall with their pink-hued lace, an extravagance worthy of pilgrimage. Dylan grins when we round the corner of an old brick classroom building and are tumbled into fairytale enchantment. Snowfall-thick, blossoms cover the grass, scattering as Dylan runs, runs laughing, runs tumbling, runs exulting.

We chase petals scuttled by the wind. We toss handfuls of petals into the air. We drop blossoms into the open palms of our hands and blow on them.

I lift Dylan onto a thick branch so that she sits enfolded in cherry blossoms. I hand her an apple that I've brought for a snack, and she bites into it, hunger enlivened by the cool spring air and by her interplay with the blossoms. I want Dylan's every sense engaged by this landscape of marvels: foam froth, and honey scent, rough bark on skin, breeze on cheek. And apple's sweet juice on tongue, lingering on lips, the taste of other enchantments, other landscapes, woven into this newly mythic land of blossoms.

That day, on our way home from the fairytale, we stop to run our hands through the blossoms on our neighborhood apple tree, echoing our play among the trees at the quad. Tucked into the blossoms, we find small, round, green, tiny, perfect spheres. "Buds?" asks Dylan, looking close. Then, startled, recognizing the face of her old friend: "Apple?"

"Yes, Dylan, apple," I affirm. "Those are tiny, tiny apples, just beginning to grow."

In this moment of recognition, apple trees step forward into the story of the green and growing things around us. Not a static tree, tree-with-fruit or tree-without-fruit, but a participant in a story of pulsing rhythms and change, a story of motion.

"Baby apple," Dylan offers, naming this tiny fruit at once familiar and never seen before.

Dylan leans into the tree's branches, fingers moving deliberately through the bright new-sprung leaves and the soft blossoms, searching, finding. She curls her hand around a baby apple, and it is just the size of her small hand.

"Baby apple." she says. "I eat it."

And she steps into the story of life unfolding always forward, never all done.

Footsteps on the Ground

Walking is the great adventure, the first meditation,
a practice of heartiness and soul.

Gary Snyder, *The Practice of the Wild*

Credit: Copyright © 1990 by Gary Snyder from *The Practice of the Wild*. Reprinted by permission of Counterpoint.

Fifty people, most of whom are meeting for the first time, gather on a July morning in a Seattle beach park on the shores of Puget Sound. They are about to set off together on The Long Walk, a four-day, 45-mile tramp through the cities, suburbs, farmlands, and forests of King County, following an interlocking system of regional bike and pedestrian trails. The purpose with this walk? "Our cause, if we have one," says Long Walk organizer Susan Robb, "is to engage geography, community, and art in a unique way, to delve into the meaning of landscape and home."

The slogan of the King County Parks is "your big backyard." On The Long Walk, participants explore that big backyard one footstep at a time. As they walk, they talk and write and make art, they forage edible and medicinal plants, they gather stories of people who live and work in the valleys and watersheds through which they pass. "Walking has a way of fostering transformation," says Robb. "By slowing down to footstep speed we become intimately connected with our home."

Walking into knowledge. Walking into home. This walking is an expression of curiosity about and reverence for the spirit and story of a particular place. It invites attentiveness to one's inward landscape as well as to the landscape traversed. Setting out, a walker carries little but curiosity and desire. Returning, a walker carries a breathing awareness of the land.

Could we walk this way in our home places? Reverent and awake, moving beyond the habitual ways of seeing the land so that the land is made new by our attention?

What new seeing, what new knowing, is possible? What marvels might we witness? The floating, rhythmic dance of a spider building a web, stitching together the handrails on a front porch. The slow gold closing of a California poppy at dusk. The ants' methodical procession across the sidewalk, carrying preposterously large crumbs from a spill of litter to a slit in the sidewalk, which they enter full-burdened and leave empty-handed, ready for another load.

Such walking offers transformation sparked by the intimacy of attention. The land is no longer anonymous, a surface landscape through which we move unseeing; it is land as a place for gladness and knowing. We leave our footprints on the land, and we carry with us its mist and dust and scent. We tell stories about our walks, stories of the spider, the poppy, the ants, stories that mark us as intimates to a place.

"We do this walk several times a week," writes Marc Parent about his efforts to make a home with his family in new terrain. "It's a way for us to load ourselves up with the feel of the landscape.

The only difference between a place to live and holy land is the number of footsteps you've put into the ground."

Time is intimacy. When we visit a landscape again and again—visit and notice, consciously, what we find there; visit and talk about what we notice—when we visit a landscape again and again, we come to know its particularities: the changes in light and shadow, the life and death of the green things, the movement of the lively things, the way rain slicks across rock and slips into dirt. Dylan and I visited a handful of places many, many times. The world narrowed to these few places—beach and meadow, creek and wetland, orchard and wooded trail. In that narrowing, the world became more subtle and nuanced, more specific. And in that specificity, the world opened into its righteous vastness: a dozen types of birds, and the whole arcing sky and its clouds, insects that burrow and buzz, trees and bush and underbrush, flowers in blossom and in seed, wild grasses and reeds and waterlilies, fish and the movement of water as creek and the movement of water as wave.

On our first day together, I tuck Dylan into a sling on my chest and step out into the neighborhood. This is new terrain for me; the morning's walk marks my first steps toward knowing this place. We meander along the sidewalks and across streets, and come eventually to a sprawling patch of blackberry canes, a tangling of green vines and sharp thorns and deep-hued fruit. I reach into the thicket, pick a blackberry, and offer it to Dylan, who obligingly pops it into her mouth. She chews lustily and gulps, then demands, "Mo!" Her first blackberry, and she's hooked.

I pick more, she eats more, her lips become purple—and her chin, and hands, and cheeks—and she eats more, until finally I cut her off.

Blackberry: "Ba-ber," in Dylan's baby dialect. A fruity passion carried forward and strengthened through the fall. Blackberry canes become landmarks along our walking routes through the neighborhood—and they become destinations in their own right. "Ba-ber!" Dylan exclaims, when she spots the distinctive tangle of canes, leaves, and fruit. Her exclamation is a command: "Stop here, and pick me some berries!"

After a few weeks of on-demand blackberries, I teach Dylan how to pick the fruit herself. Now, when we come across a blackberry bramble, I lift her close to the bushes and she leans into their thorny snarl to pluck, with delicate precision, the blue-black berries.

Through the fall and into early winter, Dylan finds berries on the bushes we pass—long beyond the point in the season when I expect to find the fruit. Dylan is a connoisseur of blackberries, directing us to the most substantive bushes in the neighborhood, peering into thickets of canes to find the last remaining edible berries. She reminds me of chanterelle mushroom hunters who move slowly through the damp forest, hunched and leaning forward, watching for a splash of yellow in the leaf litter and fern fronds, carefully filling their baskets with mushrooms more treasured than gold. "Ba-ber! Mo, mo!"

Blackberries are signposts on our walks until a dreary day in early February. That day, walking through drizzle on our way to the library, Dylan spies a blackberry thicket and bee-lines to it, calling out "Ba-ber, ba-ber!" She crouches close to the canes, searching for fruit, finding none. "Ba-ber?" she asks, calling into the canes as though hoping a berry will step forward to offer itself. "Ba-ber?" Dylan turns to me, and, gesturing toward the unresponsive canes, asks, "Ba-ber?"

"I don't see any berries on this bush, Dylan," I answer her plaintive query. "I think the blackberries are done for the winter."

"All done?" Dylan echoes, mournfully.

"Yes, sweetheart, all done. Blackberry bushes rest during the winter, so that they can make fruit again in the summer. We've had such a lot of blackberries, more than we could expect, really. But now, they're all done."

"Ba-ber all done," Dylan repeats, with one last, long look at the bramble.

Watching her sadly turn away from the bush, I think ahead to spring, when blackberry canes erupt with violet blossoms. I think of the hard green berries that form from those blossoms, slowly ripening during summer's hottest days. I imagine Dylan's autumn reunion with the tart-sweet berries, a full-circle traverse through the year.

Blackberries have become the heartbeat of this place for Dylan, the object of pilgrimage, anchor-points in the neighborhood. Now, blackberries will reveal to her the patterns of seasonal change. Dylan knows blackberries as intimates—recognizing their distinctive canes and leaves, finding her way through their green tangle to the tang of their fruit, wearing their purple stain on fingers and lips. Her particular knowledge will allow broader seeing: from the specific comes the expansive. Blackberries will become the lens through which Dylan can watch winter become spring become summer become autumn, again.

Walk the land to learn the land—its seasons and cycles, its green and growing things, the flight of birds across its sky and the creep of insects across its earth. Walk the land mindful and alert, ready to stop at each encounter with both the astonishing and the familiar.

"The childhood landscape is learned on foot," writes Gary Snyder. "A map is inscribed in the mind—trails and pathways and groves— the mean dog, the cranky old man's house, the pasture with a bull in it—going out wider and farther." These local maps, made by walking, tell a personal and particular story of a place; the map-maker and the landscape fold into each other, so that the land is brought alive by the mapping, even as the map-maker falls into the land, becoming a participant in it. This mapping lays the foundation for an ecological identity, in which a place and its ecology are inscribed in the mind. Knowing one place intimately makes possible knowledge of other places: we become adept at paying attention, we are attuned to the marvelous and beautiful.

This is what I learned, walking with Dylan, about how to inscribe a map in our minds and hearts.

I decided that Dylan and I would explore a few places, visiting them often, so that we'd come to know their details and specificities (like where the best blackberry bushes grow!) and in that way, come to know their character. This, I thought, would be better than trying to create a broad-ranging atlas. It was, I thought, a 'quality versus quantity' equation: a handful of places known intimately trumps a multiplicity of places known superficially, when our goal is ecological identity. Christopher Norment suggests that, when we pay attention in such a way, we can look at "the surface of a still pond, while at the same time becoming fully aware of the column of water beneath, the sweep and undulations of the bottom sediments, the paths traced by beetles as they move through the pond's depths." That sort of knowledge is what I wanted for Dylan.

To come to such knowledge requires more than simple visitation, of course. Visiting our few and familiar places, I practiced walking with my senses engaged, and my attention, and my curiosity and wonderment and delight. This way of walking came naturally to Dylan; it was me who had to unlearn habits of quick traverse, destination-bound, it was me who had to become adept at the skill of attentive and meandering strolling. Thoreau wrote, "I am alarmed when it happens that I have walked a mile into the woods bodily, without getting there in spirit. . . . [When] I am not where my body is, I am out of my senses. In my walks I would fain return to my senses." That wonderfully describes what I learned with Dylan: to walk with my senses awake. To notice the land in its details and its grand gestures. To talk with Dylan about what I saw, what I felt, what stirred in me in the places we frequented. And, too, to be quiet and attentive, simply letting a place saturate me.

I carried a field guide with us on our outings, but I didn't always take it out. When we encountered a creature or plant that was entirely new, I'd pull out the field guide to see what we could learn about its name and habits; then, it helped us see more deeply into a place. But there were times when I turned to the field guide too soon, or gave it too much emphasis, and turned our exploration into an instructional session. Over the months that we spent together, I became more circumspect about when and how I offered the field guide, often taking only a quick peek while we were out walking, and waiting to linger with the field guide when we arrived back home, when our reading invited us to revisit our encounter with the new and unfamiliar, and to expand our understanding of it.

There are contradictions in all this, yes: *talk and be quiet. Learn the names and marvel without knowing names.* There is no easy distillation of how to be in a place with a child. With Dylan at the blackberries, sometimes we discussed their sweet tang, sometimes we just savored the fruit, sharing purple smiles. There were times through the winter and spring when I talked with Dylan about the bushes' cycle of rest and growth; sometimes those explanations sounded like foolish jibber-jabber, and sometimes I nailed the right balance of contextualizing information. The only instruction for how to be in a place with a child, it seems to me, is to be wholeheartedly, attentively, genuinely present. Which means, sometimes, conversation and sometimes, quiet. Sometimes, naming, sometimes, marveling. Being present, together, all the time, in generous and interested relationship with each other and with a place.

Walk the land. Come to know one small patch of earth intimately. Stand on that ground until it becomes dear to you and then open your arms to the whole wide world.

References

Jordan Howland, "The Long Walk's Double Proposition:
An Interview with Susan Robb."
4Culture blog, June 4, 2012.

Christopher Norment, *Return to Warden's Grove:
Science, Desire, and the Lives of Sparrows*.
University of Iowa Press, 2008.

Marc Parent, *Believing it All: What My Children Taught Me
about Trout Fishing, Jelly Toast, and Life*.
New York: Little, Brown and Company, 2001.

Gary Snyder, "The Place, the Region, and the Commons"
in *The Practice of the Wild*.
San Francisco: North Point Press, 1990.

Henry David Thoreau. "Walking." In *The Portable Thoreau*,
Carl Bode, editor. New York: Penguin, 1979.

Practice Silence

Eagles and Salmon

The river is famous to the fish.

The loud voice is famous to silence,
Which knew it would inherit the earth
Before anybody said so.
...
The tear is famous, briefly, to the cheek.

The boot is famous to the earth,
More famous than the dress shoe,
Which is famous only to floors.

Naomi Shihab Nye, "Famous"

Excerpt from "Famous" from *Words Under the Words: Selected Poems* by Naomi Shihab Nye, copyright © 1995. Reprinted with the permission of Far Corner Books, Portland, Oregon.

On a cool October morning, Dylan and I follow a path through an old apple orchard in Magnuson Park at Lake Washington. The path tumbles us onto one of the tiny beaches that rim the park, a beach tucked into the curving arm of the land and big enough only for the two of us. Blackberry bushes and tall grass edge the beach, and a cottonwood tree overhangs it. The beach is thick with small, smooth stones, perfect for throwing into the lake.

And that's what we do, Dylan and I. We throw rocks into the water.

The day is gray and the water is flat and still. Mist shrouds the shoreline. There is just this tiny beach and the quiet water and the splash of rocks, and our laughter.

And then, a shriek! Loud and wild, from the cottonwood overhead.

Startled, Dylan looks at me, and I look up into the tree's branches. There, just above us, are two bald eagles.

My heart skips a beat. What a glory, to stand so close to these two fierce-beaked, strong-bodied raptors! I gesture to the tree, telling Dylan with excitement, "That cry is the call of eagles. There are two of them in the cottonwood tree!" Dylan peers upward for a moment, then returns her attention to the stony beach, and to the many rocks waiting to be flung into the water.

I wrestle with whether I ought to urge Dylan to attend to the eagles. To be so close to the wildness of eagles is an extraordinary thing. But the tree and the sky and the eagles quilt together in shades of gray, brown, and black; it's difficult to make out the eagles in the tree, if you don't know what to look for—and Dylan doesn't. She doesn't know 'eagle,' the word or the raptor. This is an opportunity for her to learn 'eagle,' yes, but only with some determined effort by both of us.

I decide not to force the moment. Dylan delights in her rock-throwing, and she's well-ensconced on the beach, toes right at the water's edge. I could ask her to look for the eagles in the tree, could point her toward their bright white heads as a way to identify them, could, in these ways, introduce her to eagles. But I don't know how to communicate what I really want her to know: that it is a rare and holy thing to stand beneath twin eagles. The words I would fumble my way to would be inadequate to capture the signifying grace of the eagles' presence—and, anyway, they'd be unintelligible to Dylan, only sixteen months old. There is no instruction to offer. What I can give Dylan, in this moment, is my reverence, my glad astonishment at our good fortune, my upward gaze and wordless watching.

Dylan carries on with rocks-in-the-water, laughing, calling out, "Splash! Splash!" Every few tosses, she hands me a rock: "Ann throw it," she commands, and I do, and we laugh together. And then I look up again at the eagles, memorizing their posture, the turn of their heads, the intensity of their gaze, the clutch of their talons and the curve of their beaks. Offering a silent prayer of gratitude.

A few weeks later, I take Dylan to the Cedar River for our first— and likely our only—visit there together. Each October, I make a pilgrimage to the Cedar River to witness the homecoming of sockeye salmon after their sojourn in the Pacific Ocean. This year, I am eager to share that pilgrimage with Dylan.

The Cedar River originates in the Cascade Mountains east of Seattle and, after 45 meandering miles, drains into Lake Washington, the lake where we stood beneath the eagles. The river's watershed is one of the best remaining salmon habitats in our region. Sockeye born in the Cedar River travel its watercourse to Lake Washington and, from the lake, through Seattle's Chittenden Locks into the ocean. After several years of saltwater life, the salmon retrace their journey: Locks to lake to river, returning home to lay and fertilize eggs, and, then, to die. It is an epic journey, and worthy of witness.

It's a long drive to the river, nearly an hour. Dylan and I leave first thing in the morning, and Dylan sleeps much of the way there. When we arrive at the trailhead, I wake Dylan and we bundle into our fleece jackets; the day is clear, bright with autumn sun, and cool-edged.

The trail to the river is short, and, happily, lined with blackberry canes. We feast on the last of the season's berries and arrive at the river with purple tongues and juice-stained fingers.

The trail spills us onto the riverbank where the water runs fast around a bend and across a rocky shallow. This is where the salmon spawn, this pebble-filled curve in the river. As soon as we get to the river, we hear splashing. We hurry to the water's edge to locate the source of the commotion. A salmon leaps and falls, leaps and falls, working its way up the river's frothy flow.

I lift Dylan into my arms to give her a clearer view into the water, and we both squint out at the river. I spot five deep-red and mottled-green fish in the river six feet from us, bodies turned upstream, pushing against the current's resistant muscle to move deeper into their home waters. "Look, Dylan!" I exclaim. "Salmon! Fish, swimming. Salmon." I point out the fish, hoping that Dylan can see them through the water's shimmers and folds—hoping that their shape and movement will catch her attention, so that she can begin to know salmon.

Dylan scans the river, looking where I gesture. I feel the moment when she sees the salmon; her body stiffens, there's a change in her breathing.

We stand together on the riverbank for a long time, silent and watchful. The salmon and their compelling effort have our full attention. They thrust themselves forward and are carried back by the onrushing water. Determined, they thrust again, gaining three inches, five inches—and then are swept back by the river's indifferent flow. Several salmon spin away downriver, carried by the current. Two salmon veer into the shallow water at the river's edge; one, a male, begins to wriggle into the pebbles and silt, preparing a place for his companion to deposit her eggs. Another salmon continues its wearying struggle with the river, forcing itself forward, forward, forward.

We watch them, Dylan and I, silent save for an exclamation when one of the salmon jumps and splashes. Tears rise in me. I weep at the poignant beauty of this moment, at the fleeting flaming life present here: the constancy of the river's rushing and the grandeur of the trees' autumn flare. The passage of geese overhead, announcing with their wild dissonant calls the end of the soft season and the imminence of the bleak season. And the salmon, ah, the salmon, intent and graceful and exhausted and determined.

I weep, and I worry that my tears disconcert Dylan. I try to explain:

"The salmon are swimming back to this river where they were born. They come to this river to lay eggs, and then to die." I pause, aware that this natural history lesson is inadequate and unnecessary. My words are a disruption of the moment. I shouldn't have spoken. But I finish, wanting to assure Dylan that my tears are okay, that I'm okay—not injured or frightened, simply moved. And so I add, "It's such a journey for these salmon, from the ocean to this river, and I feel tearful, watching the effort of it and the wildness of it."

Dylan is a year old; what do these words signify to her? The tone of my voice, my tears, these are what instruct her, not language. I stop talking, and we continue to watch the salmon, and my tears stop, and eventually Dylan stirs in my arms, ready to walk the trail that follows the river downstream.

Reference

Naomi Shihab Nye, "Famous." In *Words Under the Words: Selected Poems*. Portland, OR: Far Corner Books, 1995.

Reverence

There are no unsacred places:
There are only sacred places
and desecrated places.

Wendell Berry, "How to Be a Poet"

Credit: Copyright © 2005 by Wendell Berry from *Given*. Reprinted by permission of Counterpoint.

On the wall in front of me hangs the portrait, "The Grand Canyon of the Yellowstone" by Thomas Moran. Gold-hued and jagged, the canyon walls slope steeply down to the whitewater river flung to the canyon floor by a waterfall so massive that it visibly mists the air in the far-reaching distance. Moran painted this landscape in 1872; his painting of that wild land accompanied the stories that flowed east from explorers who told of geysers and canyons, glaciers and grizzly bears and hot springs rimmed white with calcium deposits—land unlike anything known on the East Coast. The painting and the stories ignited the imaginations of common folk and of Congress, and sparked the creation of Yellowstone as our country's first national park in 1872.

I encounter Moran's painting in an exhibit at the Seattle Art Museum: "Beauty and Bounty: American Art in an Age of Exploration." The paintings that fill the gallery are full of golden light, all horizon and open space edged by rugged mountains and bouldered rivers. They tell of the artists' experiences of awe in their encounters with the grandeur of the West. They are reverence made visible.

Reverence: astonishment and wonder. The word's Latin origins braid together fear and awe, caution and awareness. It is not an easy emotion. It can bring us to tears, bring us to our knees, bring us to the edge of conversion.

Definitions of reverence mention veneration, devotion. Reverence may begin in the speechlessness of pure astonishment, but it soon spills from the heart into exclamation and gesture—"Look! Listen! Notice with me!" Witness this wonderful thing—and witness my wonderment. We make a painting or a poem or a prayer. Reverence implies relationship. It is different from the passivity of awe, which immobilizes us (think of 'awestruck'); it calls us to *do* something—to revere, to show honor, to make manifest our devotion. Uplifted and humbled by our encounter with the ineffable, with the wondrous and majestic, we seek to behave in a way that is worthy of and aligned with that which we revere.

And so reverence matters. It shades how we see the world and it shapes how we move through the world. Reverence toward the natural world—its canyons and waterfalls, honeybees and hummingbirds and homecoming salmon—informs our behavior, makes conservationists out of us, unwilling to allow that which we revere to be treated with contempt.

Yes, this is a fine line of reasoning, a compelling defense of reverence. . . .

And yet:

Thomas Moran traveled to the Yellowstone River and its canyons as part of an 1871 survey to chart a course for the Northern Pacific Railroad. These sorts of survey expeditions commonly included painters and photographers with the explicit intention of engendering commerce: their organizers—railroads, land speculators and developers, mining and logging companies— counted on the paintings and photos to arouse America's hunger to cross the country and settle the West. An art editor during this period of expansion described paintings like Moran's "Grand Canyon of Yellowstone" as important because they "showed us the scenery of which we were hitherto the ignorant possessors." Ownership inspires different gestures than devotion.

Reverence bends us to our knees. When we stand again, we have to choose: How will we make our lives, now, in relationship with the marvel we've witnessed?

Reverence is more complicated than it seems.

What do the landscape photos and paintings of our times feature? Curious, I visit galleries and find endangered and vanishing places and creatures: "The Last Polar Bear," "Wolves," "Birds of the Arctic National Wildlife Refuge." Coral reefs and their otherworldly fish. The dynamics of time and place given physical form by environmental artists working with twigs and tides, with the slow topple of stones and the quick-melt of ice. Photographs of forests and loggers, of mountains and miners. This art is an elegy for defiled land, even as it strives to dignify the laborers who are wrecking the land, hard-working, poor, and enmeshed in the ruinous work of 'resource extraction.'

Photos and paintings today convey reverence for what is fragile and vanishing, and for what we long to renew. This reverence is complicated by distance in which direct encounter is replaced by imagination, and by the aching awareness of the precariousness of this Earth's beauty and bounty. It is reverence tinged by romance—the romance of wilderness, of raw places, of places that exist at the edge of loss. It is reverence offered as hope—or, perhaps, it is grief and shame speaking the language of reverence: a wish that what is beautiful will continue, a wish that we had behaved better toward the land, a wish for time and desire enough to change our ways.

What can we learn from this experience of reverence?
What does it suggest for how we call reverence into a child's life?

My dad grew up in Red Lodge, Montana, a small farming and mining town that boasts of its mile-high elevation, tucked into the Beartooth Mountains just outside of Yellowstone National Park. Red Lodge was salt-of-the-earth, made into a community by the immigrant families from Northern and Eastern Europe who'd come there to work in the mines. After mining or alongside it, they worked the land, farming it to make it home.

My dad's uncles Ted, Bluey, Vern, and Ernie farmed a hundred acres of hay and wheat, corn and peas; they kept chickens for eggs and turkeys for holiday feasts and cows for milk, cream, and butter. The farm was irrigated by small streams that tumbled through their land from the high mountains.

My dad lived in town a couple of miles from the farm. As a boy, most days after school he'd follow Willow Creek up from town to fish the streams and ponds on his uncles' land and to roam the undomesticated hillsides around the farm. He didn't grow up hiking or camping, his family didn't design intentional outdoor experiences for him and his brothers. The land was, simply, a central setting for his childhood, alongside his life in town.

My dad is 80 now, and he pines for that land—pines for those mountains and streams and farmland. He pines for it in a nostalgic way, certainly, remembering what was, and also in the way of looking back at what wasn't. "I wish I'd hiked the mountains. I wish I'd camped and climbed, paid more attention to the beauty of it all." Now, in these bookmark years counterposed to his childhood, living at some distance from those mountains, my father speaks of the land with reverence. In his boyhood, the land was unremarkably and wonderfully the land. Now, he recognizes the land's majesty—those Montana mountains, those clear-water streams that flow shallow and fast over pebbles and silt, that sky, that endless sky. He recognizes it and longs for it, and he sees the world, now, through that recognition and longing. Through that reverence, deep-felt but unvoiced as a child, given full-voice as an adult.

The writer Rick Bass—who is raising two daughters in backcountry Montana—says this about the reverence that he wishes for his children: "For as long as possible, I want them to keep believing that beauty, though not quite commonplace, and never to pass unobserved or unappreciated, is nonetheless easily witnessed on any day, in any given moment, around any forthcoming bend. Around the next bend."

This was my father's experience: Beauty around the next bend. Beauty that now, remembered, takes his breath away. Beauty that known as a child, was everyday, unremarked-on, ordinary. The ordinary extraordinary.

Beauty now made extraordinary through distance and through loss.

The farm is gone, sold during hard financial times after World War II and, soon after, subdivided into cheap housing. The creeks have gone underground or gone dry. Red Lodge Mountain is a ski resort.

It is nothing to take for granted, such wild beauty as the high Rockies offer.

How do we invite children into reverence, which is, surely, a cornerstone of an ecological identity? How do we cultivate an attitude of reverence in ourselves?

I believe that silence — space around language — is the doorway into reverence: In the presence of the majestic and marvelous, of the wondrous in its minutest detail and its fullest grandeur, we ought simply to be still.

In the quiet space around language, tears arise. And laughter. Reverence isn't necessarily sober and, well, reverential. A heron stands at the river's edge, its lavender-blue feathers riffling in the breeze, all elegant curves and grace — and then it spreads its wings and rises into the air, and squawks its comical cry, and we bust out laughing — even as we bow in gratitude to witness such beauty as a heron, as flight. We watch a spider spin its web, a meditation of precise movement—and then we watch it wrap a fly in the same silky thread and we watch the fly struggle and flail and then become motionless, and even as we marvel at the spider's dance across the web—and even though we're not in any way fond of flies—we are repulsed by the spider's eager dispatch of the living, buzzing insect. Reverence is full-feeling, emotion uncircumscribed by language.

We speak such a lot, we humans. Especially adults to children. Talk, talk, talk: we describe, we question, we instruct. We talk to exchange what we know, what we care about, the gossip of the day. When are we silent? In church, synagogue, mosque. In meditation, in yoga, in solitude. In the presence of majesty. In the experience of awe. In the face of a miracle. Which is to say, in witness to heron and spider, flight and web, storm cloud and jewel-backed beetle, blackberry and dandelion and worm.

Dylan's family spends the weekend at the beach and comes home with a newt that they found near their creek-side campsite. They fashion a little home for the newt in a clear-walled box, and, for a week—until they return the foundling to its home creek—the newt lives in a place of honor in the family room.

On the newt's first morning in the house, I pull a chair close to its windowed home, Dylan settles onto my lap, and together, we lean forward to gaze at the newt in its improvised habitat. It lies on a fist-sized rock, not doing much of anything except breathing.

We watch it lie around. We watch it breathe. It shifts its position a couple times, looks around, flicks its tongue, lies around some more. Dylan and I are mostly quiet; every so often one of us comments about something we notice: "Her tail is in the water, now." "Tongue." "Breathing."

At first, I'm waiting for something to happen. I'm running *National Geographic* footage in my mind, and watching the newt with anticipation of branch-climbing acrobatics or a life-and-death struggle with one of the insects in the box. But nothing happens. The newt just lies around and looks around, flicks its tongue and shifts its tail, and after awhile, I stop waiting and start watching, like Dylan is doing.

I look at the newt's black-brown backside, rough with tiny bumps. I look at the deep orange line that edges its body as it lies on the rock, evidence of a bold-colored belly. The newt's tail is longer than its body, I notice, and the whole creature is no more than five inches long, tail to nose. Its legs reach at right angles from its torso, and are elbowed, squared off. Three toes on each limb lightly grip the rock. Its eyes are round and bright, but small, not dominating like a frog's eyes, and this surprises me; I gaze at its eyes a long time, watching their steady observation of this foreign terrain. The newt's back rises and falls with its breath, neither fast nor slow, an easy rhythm, up and down, up and down.

The room is vastly quiet. Dylan and I have fallen silent, no longer commenting on what we notice. This moment is saturated with attention; the room feels dense and thick, like the air on a muggy day.

That is my experience of this half-hour with the newt.

What is this encounter for Dylan? She leans forward, her body is still, her gaze is steady. What does she see? Is she making mental connections to other creatures? Interpreting the newt's behavior? Absorbing details, imprinting this newt on her mind? She has been watching and watching—she didn't start out waiting for anything, like I did: that's my assumption, anyway, and I think I'm right. What does she know to wait for? This newt, an astonishing and completely new creature, is worthy of full attention in its own right, and that's what Dylan is offering it, her full attention. Her silent and watchful presence. Her reverence.

Watching a newt for a half-hour of its life, for a half-hour of our lives. What is such respect, but reverence?

Kathleen Jamie writes about her experience as a birder: "This is what I want to learn: to notice, but not to analyze. To still the part of the brain that's yammering, 'My god, what's that? A stork, a crane, an ibis?' Sometimes we have to hush the frantic inner voice . . . and learn again to look, to listen. You can do the organizing and identifying later, but right now, just be open to it, try to see the colour, the unchancy shape—hold it in your head, bring it home intact."

That's what Dylan was doing: bringing the newt home intact.

Young children may be better positioned for witness, for looking and listening and noticing, than we adults—more adept at giving-over to an encounter with something wondrous. They don't have much formal language, nor, often, any particular knowledge of the things that they encounter—the newt, the eagle, the bee in the sunflower. Words don't get in the way of experience, not in that first year or two of life.

We adults are quick to infuse words into encounter. We are conscious of our reverence and of the contextualizing story around each encounter: the newt's true home in a pebbled stream, the problematic dislocation of an animal from its native land, the natural history of its living and dying, its conservation status, its diet. We are eager to pass on our stories and our knowledge and our questions, our values and convictions. We tumble quickly from silence into speech and, tumbling, we slip away from reverence and fall into instruction. Environmental education, natural history, directives for ecological behavior: these have essential places in shaping and sustaining an ecological identity, but they ought not to be our first gesture in the presence of a miracle.

In the presence of a miracle, astonishment. Dazzlement. Delight beyond words. Beyond words: silence. Not sober and staid, not necessarily. But beyond words. Witness and wonder.

Later, words. First, reverence.

References

Rick Bass, *The Wild Marsh: Four Seasons at Home in Montana*.
New York: Houghton Mifflin Harcourt, 2009.

Wendell Berry, "How to Be a Poet," in *Given*.
Berkeley, CA: Counterpoint Press, 2005.

Kathleen Jamie, *Findings: Essays on the Natural and Unnatural World*.
St. Paul, MN: Graywolf Press, 2005.

Seattle Art Museum curator's notes for
"Beauty and Bounty: American Art in an Age of Exploration."

Learn the Names

Bird Year

It is most humbling to sit among the birds. I will take them as my mentors.
They teach me to be still, to be patient and listen, to observe, to be able
to discern when to build nests and of what, when it is time to migrate
and when it is time to settle. They show me how to hide and how
to be seen. Feather by feather, they instruct through beauty, when
to sing and when to forage and what is learned inside the egg.
They remind me that we too can navigate by stars.

Terry Tempest Williams, *Leap*

Dylan and I sit on bags of bird seed stacked in a corner of the
Audubon gift shop. We're reading through a pile of field guides
to choose one to take home with us. We exclaim at birds we
recognize, call out their names, sound their calls:

"Robin! Cheerily—cheer-up, cheerily—cheer-up . . ."

"Caw-caw! Crow!"

"Gull! Eeeeeeeee—eeee."

"Chickadee." "Great blue heron." "Sparrow."

Reading the field guide, we retrace our year together, birds as
touchpoints. I remember our first meetings with each of these
birds—all but the crow, who Dylan already knew well when our
year began. The birds and our coming to know them tell the

story of this year, and of this place. Birds as witness, birds as companions, birds as biographers.

Matthews Beach, October 30

Mist floats on the water and fog blurs the edges of the park, erasing everything but the lake and the grassy meadow and the autumn-hued trees that ring the meadow. Just out from the shore, there is a flotilla of birds—50? 60? 75?—dark against the slate gray water: ducks, cormorants, gulls, coots. Dylan and I walk to the water's edge to watch the birds. Dylan stands very still, eyes locked on the birds floating off-shore.

A group of ducks break away from the flotilla. They make their way to the grassy meadow just beyond us. Dylan turns, quick and sure, to follow them, calling out to them in her crow-rough voice: "Caw! Caw-caw!" They quack and waddle their way to the center of the meadow, where a handful of gulls join them. The ducks graze: the sound of them pulling up grass and rooting out insects gradually fills the meadow. Dylan stands in the middle of the band of ducks and gulls and watches, unmoving and quiet. Then, a gull strides off across the grass and Dylan leaps into motion, following it with a loud, laughing whoop and a "Caw! Caw!"

The gull stays just ahead of her, leading her up the meadow to the trees at the meadow's edge and then back into the green grass. Dylan chortles as she follows, and calls out, again and again, "Caw-caw! Caw! Caw!"

The gull eventually spreads its wings and launches itself into the air with one shrill cry. Its slow-motion grace carries it over Dylan's head and back to the birds on the grass behind her. Dylan cries out as it flies just beyond her up-reaching arms, mimicking this newly-heard bird call: "Eeeeee—eeeee!" Then she makes her way back into the center of the grazing group of ducks and gulls, and mills around with them, following one, then another, squatting to touch the grass, to pull at the grass, bending forward so she can tongue the grass . . . 15 minutes, 20 minutes, 25 minutes, Dylan grazes with the ducks.

Then a dog bounds into the meadow, and the birds rise, as one body, into the air, calling out in a cacophony of irritation and alarm; gulls and mallards fly across the meadow, across the beach, onto the lake, where they land all skates and splashes and tumult, before quieting into the water and floating. . . .

And Dylan—as the birds rise around her, fly over her, stir the air around her with their wings and shrieking cries—Dylan stretches toward them, head raised, arms raised, voice raised with their voices.

A week later, at the Burke Museum

Such a rainstorm, the first of our November monsoons, the sort of rain that floods the rural rivers and that rivers the urban streets. Such rain as Dylan hasn't yet experienced: Walking to the bus this morning, she touched her wet cheek and murmured, "Water," held out her wet hand and marveled, "Water," stroked my dripping hair and asked, "Water?" A good day for a museum.

The Burke Museum of Natural History and Culture temporarily hosts "Winged Migrations," an exhibit that seems fitted for Dylan, who is a devoted student of birds. I take Dylan to the museum as provocation and as affirmation, curiosity honored and stretched into new terrain.

At the museum, we strip off our sodden coats and hats and hang them to drip in the coat rack in the foyer; then we enter the museum proper. There, Dylan stops abruptly, halted in her forward-tilting gait. A wall-sized photo of an Arctic tern hangs across from us. Dylan stares at the photo, then turns to me wide-eyed and draws on her rudimentary "sign language for babies" vocabulary to make the ASL sign for 'BIRD.' She shivers her whole body in the way she does when she's especially excited. We walk close to the wall where the tern is frozen in flight, and study the image: the spread of the bird's wings, the curve and point of its beak, the way the sky opens around the tern and the land is left behind.

After a few minutes of silent study, Dylan turns to the rest of the exhibit, a dozen photos of Arctic birds all enlarged to astounding size. I lift Dylan up close to the photos and step back with her from the photos, shifting our perspective on the birds. We comment on the photos, linking them to birds we've seen together: "The loon in this photo reminds me of the cormorants we saw floating on the lake at Matthews Beach; remember them, with the gulls and mallards?" "Quack! Quack. Eeeee-eeee."

"The jaeger is plucking at the tall grass in the same way that the crows sometimes do."

"Caw-caw!" with a bob of her head like a crow stabbing into grass. We make the full circuit of the exhibit room, looking, talking, looking, and then we move around the corner and are face to face with the Arctic tern again, this time not in silent awe, but with an outpouring of sound: Dylan begins to call her shrieking gull-cry: "Eeeeee-eeee. Eeeee-eeee." Over and over, standing face to face with the dramatically larger-than-life tern, Dylan calls to it, pausing every few cries as though listening for a response, then calling again: "Eeeeee-eeee. Eeeee-eeee." Then a final pause, and another hand-sign, thumb and pointer finger shaped like a beak, held at her cheek: "BIRD," she signs, and "Eeeeee-eeee," she calls.

Through the spring, new birds, named and known by call

Three robins perch on a tree limb. "Crow?" "Nope, those birds aren't crows. They're . . . "

"Eeeee-eee?" "Nope, those birds aren't gulls, either. They're robins."

"Rrrobbinn," emphasizing the strong consonants that make a robin so solid and reliable. We listen to the robins' song: "Chee-chee-chee, chee-chee," up and down in a rhythmic lilt, and Dylan begins to mimic it. And Dylan's mimicry inspires me to listen with new ears and to try my own echo of the robin's song: "Chee-chee-chee, chee-chee." And there we stand, Dylan and the robins and me, calling to each other, and laughing, and naming: "Chee-chee-chee." "Rrrobbinn."

Dylan on a log in a stream; a chickadee in a tree above the stream. The chickadee leaps from branch to branch, calling out, "Chickadee-dee-dee." Dylan stands still and silent, log-bound in a fast-flowing stream, tracking the bird's quick movement, listening, and, after a few minutes, singing back to the bird: "Chickadee-dee-dee!" I grin and introduce Dylan to this bird's name. She wrestles that name onto her tongue: "Chk-chk-ak."

At an urban bus stop, birds line the telephone wire overhead. "Crow?" Dylan asks. "Pigeons," I answer. Just then, the pigeons launch themselves off the wire in a unified explosive arc, tumbling into the air, circling, circling, the flurry and beat of their wings like a rush of wind. They speed away, bunched in a tight cluster, black silhouettes against a gray sky.

"Pigeon." Dylan tries this new name.

"Pigeon," I affirm. "Another type of bird. Crow, seagull, mallard, robin, chickadee. Pigeon."

Summer: Lake Washington

A mallard stands at the water's edge. Waves lap at her orange feet. She tucks her bill under her wing and shakes her head, tousling her feathers.

Dylan tilts her head toward her arm and shakes it.

The mallard lifts a foot to her face and scratches her cheek.

Dylan lifts her arm to her face and rubs it quickly back and forth across her cheek.

The mallard slowly extends one wing and one leg.

Dylan tilts onto one leg and lifts her other leg off the ground, reaching her arm to the side.

The mallard shakes her whole body, top to bottom, in a big fluff of feathers, then slips into the water, takes a drink, and drifts away down the shoreline.

Dylan shakes her whole body, then sighs. "Like a mallard," she says, watching the duck swim away.

At the Audubon shop, I choose a field guide that I think will work well for Dylan. It has photo illustrations instead of sketches, and a solid description of each bird's particular places and habits. It's a real field guide, for committed birders, which Dylan has become, attuned to the sound and movement of birds, not as a hobby but as a way of moving through the world—a way to get her bearings, to orient herself. Birds are kin, birds are teachers.

Other folks find their way through the world by learning the native trees or the flowers, or the shapes and flow of clouds, or the names and seasons of fish that swim in the local streams or the dance of the streams themselves. There is a field guide waiting for each of us that tells the story of the places we live and of our living there. These field guides become our biographies.

In conversation with terns. Singing with chickadees. "Overjoyed by a sparrow. This is exactly the kind of person I want to be." —Sharman Apt Russell

References

Sharman Apt Russell, *Standing in the Light: My Life as a Pantheist*.
New York: Basic Books, 2008.

Terry Tempest Williams, *Leap*.
New York: Vintage Books, 2001.

Naming and Knowing

An enthusiastic hiker, I was, for many years, uninterested in learning the names of things that I encountered on my frequent treks into the mountains.

I hiked hungrily up green-grown trails dense with bracken and bush and braided into the sky with up-reaching trees. I switchbacked across meadows bright-painted with wildflowers and clambered across rock fall that was sometimes a shimmer of silver and white, sometimes mottled gray and black, sometimes shaded pink and red and crimson. I ranged over mountain ridges intoxicated by the wide-horizon vistas of mountain peaks. Birds sang, critters scampered, insects buzzed by day and sang by night. But I didn't know the names of any of this liveliness. I was mildly curious, but my curiosity wasn't strong enough to propel me to learning. I wasn't particularly connected to the Cascade Mountains where I hiked; I traversed the landscape relishing the physical effort and strength, the exertion and achievement, but the land was a backdrop for my hiking rather than a place to know in its own distinct and named dimensions. The evergreen trees and blossoming wildflowers, the peaks that divide the state's east and west, were embellishments along a trail. Learning their names, I imagined, would be a chore, a tedious exercise in memorization, and not necessary for my enjoyment of this landscape.

Then, I traveled to the red rock desert of southeast Utah. That terrain, wildly different from the lush green Pacific, compelled me. I'd thought it would be beautiful, and that the challenge of backpacking there would be energizing—but I hadn't expected my heart to break open. The rock and sage, heat and dust and stars, the open sky and endlessly labyrinthing red rock canyons excited me. Now, I wanted names.

I bought my first field guide and poured over it like a love letter.
I wanted to know everything about the red rock desert, including
the names that held its stories. In the desert, I was not content
with 'rocks' and 'lizards.' I wanted details, intimacies, particular
knowledge of this particular place. Jackrabbits and kangaroo rats.
Geckos. Sidewinders. Cactus wrens, desert larks, golden eagles.
I learned the names, and each name carried me more deeply into
the desert.

This Earth is not an anonymous place. We speak of it in
generalities, using categorical names to describe what we
encounter: 'a bird,' 'a bug,' 'a rock.' In our seeing and our speaking,
we are willing to make do with broad, indistinct groupings that
contain a wide range of individuals, unacknowledged in their
particularities. The absence of names becomes a barrier to
intimacy: a bird is a bird is any bird, not this cliff sparrow,
not this crag martin. When we don't know what we see,
who we hear, where we walk, we don't know, really, where
we are. Names are integral to relationship.

I hold Dylan at her bedroom window that looks out at the
neighbors' houses across the street, and beyond those houses,
at roofs cascading downhill to Lake Washington. The lake is ringed
by a narrow strip of green and, in a broader sweep, by the orderly
angles and lines of buildings. Beyond the lake, in the far distance,
is the steady presence of the blue-hued Cascades, and, beyond the
mountains, sky and sky and sky.

It's early afternoon, and Dylan and I stand at her window for the
daily ritual that marks the end of our morning out in the world and
that turns Dylan toward her afternoon's nap.

I start, saluting the place we've spent the morning today: "Goodnight, Lake Washington."

Dylan repeats my salutation: "Night-night, Lake Washington." Then she adds her own acknowledgements, layering story, encounter, relationship onto the land: "Night-night, rocks-in-water, splash! Night-night, mallards."

"Yes," I say. "Goodnight, mallards."

"Night-night, baby ducklings."

"And goodnight, coots."

"Night-night, gulls. Night-night, crows."

On and on, the names that echo with the stories of our morning, until our final salutations.

"Goodnight, Dylan."

"Night-night, Ann."

As we create this litany of names, I think of the Hindu practice of Kirtan, the communal call-and-response chanting of the many names of the Hindu gods and goddesses. The aim of Kirtan is to carry practitioners closer to the divine; through repeating the names of the holy ones, practitioners become one with them.

Rocks, mallards. Coots, gulls, crows. Dylan. Ann.

The holy has many names.

Names are complicated. Names are a way into relationship and they grow from relationship. It's not enough to know the name of a place or a being—that doesn't make intimacy. But without knowing a name, intimacy is more difficult; it's hard to imagine caring for someone and not asking that person's name. When we do learn the name of a being or a place, it becomes more real, more filled-in, more three-dimensional and particular.

There are philosophical, cultural, and folkloric traditions that speak of 'true names'—names that express the true nature of a thing or being. Knowledge of a 'true name'—distinct from the everyday 'use name'—gives the speaker of the name special connection to, and, even, power over that thing or being. Think of Rumpelstiltskin, and the (nameless) girl released from the power of that elfish creature when she discovers his true name. Or Bilbo Baggins, in Tolkien's *The Hobbit*, whose life-and-death riddling, first with Gollum, then with the dragon Smaug, involves knowledge of true names—including his own name. Names bind speaker and named, and in that intimate connection, there is power.

Another gesture in the power of names: the knowledge of names binds a community together. When we hold in common the names of the places where we live, and the names of the beings that live there with us, we can speak together of our life in these places with these creatures. Our conversations have depth and nuance, they are particular in their details. These conversations knit us together as people-in-place. Dylan and I can speak to each other of the coots at the lakeshore where we toss rock after rock into the waves—and we can speak to other locals who know this beach and these coots, who have stood on this rocky shoreline and squinted into the sun-bright water to watch the coots paddle past, who have delighted, like us, in their rubber-duck squeak and in their charming white bills.

This particularity of shared language becomes a dialect for care. We need to know what we're talking about if we are to steward it. "Birds at the lake" doesn't give us anything to hold onto. The seasonal movement of coots along the north shore of Lake Washington is specialized knowledge; and, in the dialect of that knowledge, we can begin to talk about changes in that seasonal movement. We can use that language to wonder at the causes of those changes, and to speak publicly about the relationship between urban living and the lives of coots. Names become doorways for conservation.

Psychologist and naturalist Elaine Brooks says that, "People are unlikely to value what they cannot name."

What do we want to value? Name it.

Richard Louv reports that a 2002 study found that the average eight year old in the United States was better able to identify characters from Pokémon than the native species in the communities where they lived. I wanted Dylan to value pine trees and penstemen more than Picachu. I learned the names. I taught Dylan the names. Not right away, not in place of experience and simple, delighted wonderment. But eventually, I offered the names of the trees and birds, the flowers and shells that we encountered. Catkins and clover, seagull and sea star, apple tree and blackberry cane and thimbleberry. Names brought the Earth alive, and us in it.

When do we teach children the names of things? Not at the outset of time outdoors, nor as a substitute for it. Not from the hope that learning the names of things and creatures will create a feel for life-in-place or a reverence for a particular plot of land and its small, tender creatures. Not as environmental instruction. We offer the names of places and creatures, of growing things and living things, in the context of relationships.

Barry Lopez writes: "The quickest door to open in the woods for a child is the one that leads to the smallest room, by knowing the name each thing is called. The door that leads to the cathedral is marked by a hesitancy to speak at all, rather to encourage by example a sharpness of the senses. If one speaks it should only be to say, as well as one can, how wonderfully all this fits together, to indicate what a long, fierce peace can derive from this knowledge."

From encounter, relationship. From relationship, names. With children, we create opportunities for encounter, and we watch for the connections that are beginning to bind a child to a moment, to a creature, to a place. We watch for playful delight, for wide-eyed awe, for a body tilted forward, for a hand out-reached. We watch for the turn of a child's head toward us, and wonderment in her expression. And, then, we offer a name to illuminate a relationship already begun.

"Goodnight, cactus wren."
"Goodnight, desert lark."
"Goodnight, red rock canyon."

References

Elaine Brooks, quoted in Richard Louv, *Last Child in the Woods: Saving our Children from Nature-Deficit Disorder*. Chapel Hill, NC: Algonquin Books, 2005.

Barry Lopez, "Children in the Woods." In *Crossing Open Ground*. New York: Vintage Books, 1989.

Richard Louv, *Last Child in the Woods: Saving our Children from Nature-Deficit Disorder*. Chapel Hill, NC: Algonquin Books, 2005.

Embrace Sensuality

First Snow

Mid-December, snow in the forecast. I spend the night with Dylan to give her parents an overnight away from home to celebrate a birthday. Dylan is asleep early, tucked into the bed that we'll share; I stay up late reading next to the window, hoping for snow, a rare treat in this temperate climate. I grew up in Eastern Washington, where winters are bolder, more defined; snow-transformed landscapes are among my earliest memories. I miss the snow, living in Seattle; I feel its absence, and grow over-eager when snow is in the forecast.

Eventually, I give up my snow vigil and crawl into bed next to Dylan feeling cheated, snow only a tease. I sleep lightly, unused to sleeping with a child. In my frequent wakings, I listen to Dylan breathe, attentive to the rhythmic inhale and exhale, and to the pauses between each breath. My watchfulness becomes a way of tending to her even as she sleeps, an instinct to caregiving that makes the wakefulness a pleasure.

Listening to Dylan breathe, a vigil.

Watching for snow, a vigil.

And snow begins to fall.

And breath's whisper and snow's fall become meditations in the quiet dark.

And the quiet dark slowly gives way to first light, and the snowfall stops, and Dylan wakes.

I wrap her in a sleep-warm blanket and carry her to the window. We look out over Lake Washington and to the Cascade Mountains beyond, where the sun has begun its rising, streaking the sky gold and orange-pink. We watch the curve of the sun press into the sky, arcing up until the full sphere tumbles from behind the mountains into the clear blue morning and flames the lake gold.

This drama compels our attention—but once the sun is seated in the sky, I whisper to Dylan, "Look, sweetheart, snow."

This is Dylan's first snow. What does she see, I wonder, there at the window looking out at grass and sidewalk, tree and street, transformed? She didn't see the snow fall; she knows only falling asleep in a familiar world and waking to the world fundamentally changed. What meaning does she make of it? Snow as upwelling from the earth, the trees, the sidewalk and street? Snow as a draining of color, or as a whitewash overlay? A mask? A blanket? What meanings can Dylan make without knowing the story of snow and its fall from the sky? Is she concerned with meaning, or is she absorbed in a purely sensual encounter with snow?

Dylan and I pull on layers of clothes, slide our feet into our boots, and go out into the cold of snow on skin, the crunch and pack of it underfoot, and the powdered soft of it breezed in the bright air.

I carry Dylan down the porch steps and set her at the edge of the snowy yard. I am ready to romp in the snow. Eager to share with Dylan the lightheartedness I feel in the snow, the giddy playfulness carried from childhood to this moment. Eager to share this snow, child-like, with a child.

But Dylan is not eager. She doesn't jump into the snow to romp and play. She stands unmoving where I set her down, staring at the snow.

I coax her: "Come into the snow with me!"

Only Dylan's eyes move, flicking from the snow on the ground to my face, back and forth, looking for clues to help her understand what's happened to her familiar world, clues to guide her about how to move through this uncharted landscape.

I flash on her first day in 'real' shoes, shoes with soles and laces, not pliable baby moccasins but rigid and sturdy shoes for walking. That morning, Dylan stood staring at her feet, immobilized by the shoes' unyielding form, by their weight, their foreignness. Her body at the snow's edge, today, carries that same consternation and alertness, the tension of not knowing how to navigate such wildly unfamiliar terrain.

I coax some more, stepping out into the snow, touching my fingers to it. "We can walk in the snow," I say to Dylan. "We can touch it. You can stand with me, here in the snow."

Dylan looks at me and shakes her head. "No-no," she says. "No-no." Her voice echoes the phrasing and intonation that she uses when a dog bounds too close to her, or when a duck thrusts its head toward her hand looking for food: "No-no."

And so I wait, and Dylan waits—or endures my waiting. Five minutes . . . eight minutes . . . ten minutes. I set aside my impatient excitement about the snow and watch Dylan watching the snow.

After long and cautious study, Dylan takes a small, careful step. She lifts one foot and sets it into the snow, then pauses, getting the feel of it underfoot. Slowly, she moves her other foot forward: her first step into snow.

And then: another measured, slow-motion step. And then language, trying this new word on her tongue. "Snow," Dylan whispers. "Snow."

She touches the snow with a mittened hand. And I pull off her mittens so that she can feel the dry cold powder. I scoop up snow in my hand and lift it to my tongue, taking its cold wet tastelessness into my mouth. I offer Dylan a palmful of snow to taste; eyes wide, she touches the snow with her tongue.

Then, at last!, we walk into the snow, making footprints and pathways. We hit snow-draped bushes with sticks and watch the snow tumble and glitter. We eat snow.

For Dylan, this snow is unlooked-for, unimagined. It remakes the familiar landscape.

For me, this snow is long-anticipated, woven into memory and body's knowledge of the world.

For Dylan, a first encounter. For me, snow made new by Dylan's fresh seeing.

Full-bodied Participation

The flavors of the peach and the apricot are not lost from generation to generation. Neither are they transmitted by book-learning.

Ezra Pound, quoted in Gary Snyder, *The Practice of the Wild*

Oh, a ripe peach in August! Think of it: its full, sweet roundness; its firm, yielding flesh; its furred, rose-hued, earth-scented skin. The sugared stickiness of its juice dripped and dried on your chin, on the back of your hand. Its lingering silky taste in your mouth.

A ripe peach in August is a sensual experience.

That sensuality has been, for many of us, bound together with memory and meaning. For me, peaches evoke the feel of my childhood kitchen at the peak of summer's heat, where my mom and I peeled and sliced boxfuls of peaches, filling Mason jars with their golden half-rounds and then racking the jars in the boiling water of the canner on the stove. Those canned peaches carried us through the monochromatic winters, bright reminders of sunglow and summer-brown skin. They had their own flavor, a distant cousin to the taste of a fresh, ripe peach, but, still, they were peaches, summertime's totem, and, so, relished.

That is my peach memory, held dearly in heart and mind.

My peach knowledge is held in my body. If you've not bitten into a round, ripe peach, not taken its scent, its flavor, its fuzz-edged, slick-smooth flesh into your body, then words describing a peach don't mean much. Peach is body-knowledge, sense-knowledge.

So is the knowledge of the sharp slice of a knife, the heat of boiling water and its steam, the tightening of a metal lid onto a glass jar, and its muscled release months later. Our bodies, our senses, open the world to us.

What do you know of this wide-ranging world? Make a list, starting with the temperature of the air on your cheek as you read this, and the weight of these pages in your hands, and the scent of book ink and paper. Make a list, and feel how it carries you wide-awake into this moment of your life. Make a list, casting further into your body for knowledge—the warm embrace of bathwater, the stumble of a missed stair, the moon's glow on your nighttime pillow, the heat that escapes when an oven door is opened. Feel how that list awakens your body, leaves it alert and self-conscious and anchored in the physical world.

What a revelation it would be if we could recall our first encounters with the natural world: first snow, first peach, first crow, first stars, first sunflower—experiences before words, before stories or folktale or myth, before family history, before memory. Each encounter was a mystery, a marvel, all our senses reaching to gather information, minds busy sorting data, seeking connections to what was already-known. I think of Dylan's first summertime windstorm, trees full-leaved and alive with the wind. Listening to the rustle and flash of the leaves, Dylan groped for understanding: "Water?" she wondered, hearing echoes of the neighborhood stream in the movement of the trees.

We invoke that freshness of encounter as adults: "Imagine that you're seeing this for the first time!" we say: an admonishment to pay attention and be curious, to engage all our senses, to open ourselves fully to the wonder and astonishment that the beyond-human world deserves.

In a poignant counterpoint, we also challenge ourselves to "imagine that we'll never see this again." It's the same injunction: "Be here now. Don't let this moment pass without your full participation in it."

First encounter: wonderment. Final encounter: reverence. First and final invoked to ensure that every encounter is full-bodied.

We adults tend to be squeamish about our bodies, carefully managing our scents and secretions, our hungers and desires. Not children. They live in their bodies.

Dylan didn't necessarily relish getting her hands mucky; she wasn't a kid who flung herself unreservedly into every physical encounter. Her gestures were sometimes delicate, her exploration sometimes tentative. But, first and foremost, she engaged the world with her body, never substituting talk for experience. On any day that hinted at warmth, she tossed her jacket aside—and on any day that was actually balmy, she peeled off the rest of her clothes, as well. She went barefoot whenever I allowed it. She picked up stones and leaves and twigs, jumped into mud, dipped her fingers into rainwater run-off along the curb. She ate with her hands and didn't concern herself with smears of food on her cheeks. She picked her nose and studied her diaper's contents and laughed when she farted. She lived unabashedly in her body, all senses on call.

When I began my year with Dylan, I thought myself attuned
to the physical world, ready to bend close to a flower to study
its depths, or to pause on a walk to listen to a bird's song.
But my attention was short-lived, I learned, when Dylan was
my companion. She lingered long in her looking and listening,
crouching low to watch an ant cross the sidewalk, or standing
under the telephone wire with her head cocked back listening
to a crow's raucous calls. Dylan took such a lot of time with each
encounter, belying the notion that young children have short
attention spans. I've seen a hundred crows, and countless ants,
and I'd stopped paying them any serious attention; but for year-
old Dylan, each crow, each ant was worthy of her full attention,
a marvel of movement, of sound and silence, unpredictable and
compelling. I learned from Dylan the meaning of the oft-spoken
adage that we ought to look at the world the way a child looks,
"as if for the first time," and, so, I slowed down—way, way, down—
and started paying attention to ants and crows and their kin.

Dylan also demonstrated how to step into the rain without
hunching against the wet; how to lift a raindrop from coat sleeve
and balance it, a shimmering globe, on tongue's tip; how to invite
the full impact of food by breathing in its scent with long, deep,
sniffs. Dylan demonstrated how to participate physically and
heartily in the world.

I didn't start behaving like Dylan—I didn't start burying my nose
in my lunch and licking raindrops off my coat. But I certainly
relaxed more fully into my body, and, more importantly, I learned
to give Dylan ample permission to bring every sense into her
encounters with the world.

I became determined to leave abundant time for Dylan to physically engage the world. I believed that my role was to hold open the space for her sensory explorations—not to try to be like her, a faux-child with hands in a mud puddle and teeth clenched into a false smile, nor to force sensory exploration out of a misguided enthusiasm for physical learning: "touch this fuzzy willow bud, damn it." I wanted my invitations to Dylan to be genuine, and my own explorations authentic, motivated by my curiosity rather than by a resolve to "be a good model" for Dylan.

During this brief, sweet time of her life when she was not yet constrained by social norms about physical expression and exploration, I wanted to offer Dylan the whole world to experience with her whole body.

"Touch the flower and lean forward to smell it, maybe touch it with your lips," says Georgia O'Keefe. Yes! Take the flower onto your tongue. Hold it to your cheek. Brush its petals against the softness of your ear. Lose yourself in its nuanced color. Take the flower into your body.

Five senses illuminate the world for us: taste, touch, smell, sight, and sound. Neuroscientists add five more senses: temperature, kinesthetic sense, balance, pain, acceleration. Other current nominees for consideration as senses are time, direction, and thirst.

Our senses take in the world so that we can learn the world; they provide data for perception. And what is perception?

The understanding of the environment that we gain by our interpretations of sensory information, says the dictionary. The word 'perception' comes from the Latin *percipere*, "to seize entirely, to grasp." It shares linguistic origins with the Latin *perceptio*, meaning 'comprehension.' Our senses inform our knowing, not in a superficial way, but knowing as comprehending, which is to say, understanding the meaning and nature of a thing, understanding a thing as part of a larger whole. Our embodied participation in the world makes possible an intimate relationship with the world, and knowledgeable residence in the world.

There is a loop that happens between perception and knowledge; our sensory encounters with the natural world wire our brains for further perception. I don't fully understand the neurological science, but what I do understand fascinates me: when we look long and intently at something, our physical capacity for sight is strengthened, and that physical capacity increases our ability to see that thing again, in detail. The visual scientist Laura Sewall explains:

> *"What a person looks at a lot is analogously buried in the brain. As the neural connections become increasingly facilitated, the thing seen becomes more readily seen in subsequent open-eyed moments. . . . If we are paying attention, the thing seen will be picked up faster and with more detail and vibrancy and it will be the groundwork for a different way of seeing, and consequently, for a certain quality of mind."*

We can use our in-born sense of sight to influence how our minds work. We can teach ourselves to perceive—to see detail and subtleties—and, so, instill in our minds the disposition to know, and, knowing, to value. Sewall again:

"Such shifts in perceptual capacity—or rather, the recovery of our finely evolved sensory abilities—feed forward into shifts in consciousness. With an eye tuned to pattern, movement, beauty, and the secret lives of birds and bees, the world brightens and beckons, and what one values becomes a matter of where one stands, literally, and of the wilder and complex relations there."

This, then, is why embodied, sensual encounters with the natural world matter. Our sensual engagement with the natural world is a way of participating in that world, a way of expanding our knowledge of the places we live, and, so, knowing where we live, of caring for where we live. This is, most essentially, a definition of ecological literacy: delighted, curious, and marveling attention to the beyond-human world that opens into the experience of kinship with that world, the experience of belonging to and in a place. "Natural history requires focused attention on the distinctive patterns of flowers, birds, reptiles, social behavior, food webs, and habitats," observes Sewall. "Over time, these observations surely become a significant way of knowing the world. . . . Natural historians thus find themselves embedded in a saturated world of other beings. Consequently, they know their places deeply and deliberately, and as a further consequence, they know what they value. They tell me that they love this Earth and that joy comes easily. This is no surprise to me. With eyes and ears so highly tuned, they are undoubtedly within a phenomenologically deep world of all-the-relations."

This is what I wanted for Dylan: embodied participation, full-hearted knowing, delighted belonging on the Earth.

How to arrive there: Look. Listen. Taste. Touch. Smell.

References

Georgia O'Keeffe, from the exhibition catalogue for
"An American Place," 1939.

Ezra Pound, quoted in Gary Snyder, *The Practice of the Wild.*
San Francisco: North Point Press, 1990.

Laura Sewall, "Seeing the Natural History Way."
The Journal of Natural History Education and Experience.
Volume 5: 2011.

Explore
New Perspectives

Life and Death

September is unusually warm, and Dylan and I make frequent visits to the beach, glad to extend summer. On one of these sunny beach days, Dylan and I arrive at the water's edge to find a school of tiny fish just off-shore. The fish popcorn in and out of the water, leaping and falling, leaping and falling; their silver flash and bright spark shimmer the water and the air. As we watch, dazzled and delighted, the fish tumble their way into the shallows within wading-reach of us.

Laughing at their splashing dance, Dylan and I wade into the water with the fish.

One step, two, three steps into the water. We move close to the fish. Four steps—and the whole school, as one body, quick-slips sideways and away from us a yard or two. They're still leaping and splashing, still riffling the water and sparkling the air, and we move, again, toward them. The fish make another sideways shift, and we laugh and laugh. We play several rounds in this slow-motion game of chase, herding the fish around the shallows, following them farther and farther into the water until, soon, I'm carrying Dylan because the water's too deep for her.

And, then, the water becomes too deep for me, too, and the fish are victors in our game. They leap their way across the water away from us until we can't see them anymore.

This is Dylan's first encounter with fish—with the idea of fish and with the physical reality of fish. And what a first encounter! Dylan and I talk about it to each other and to her family, telling the story again and again over the following days: "Fish splash!" "We waded out to the fish, but when we got close, they swam away." "Fish swim!" "We followed them until we had to stand on our toes in the water, and then the water was too deep for us, and the fish swam away." "Water. Fish. Splash!"

My childhood memories of fish are of dead fish at fish markets, all gaping mouths and glassy eyes, red flesh visible in slashes in their silver skin. Or fish that were more shadow than lively presence, fish that darted away from me low under the water in the lakes where I swam as a child. What different memories Dylan will have, what a different introduction to fish! Fish as playmates, as spark and dance and laughter. I'm grateful for this chance encounter, and glad to tell and re-tell the story with Dylan.

We return to the beach the next week. As we walk through the wetland trail that takes us to the lake, we talk about the fish. "Do you suppose we'll see the fish again, Dylan? It was such fun to play with them last time we were here." "Fish. Water. Swim. Splash!" "I wonder why they were jumping and tumbling. . . ."

Chatting about the fish, we arrive at the water's edge where a sparkle on the waves three or four yards out in the lake catches my attention. I'm astounded; is it possible that the fish are here again?

Dylan sees the shimmer on the water, too. "Fish!" she exclaims, eager but not surprised. Fish have become part of the story of this beach; why would they not be waiting here for us?

We squint into the bright water. The silver shimmering thing moves steadily closer, until it's near enough that we can see it—yes! one of the tiny fish we'd played with so exuberantly last week.

But this fish is not leaping or splashing. It lies limp and loose on the water's surface, unmuscled.

This fish is dead.

But Dylan doesn't know that. She doesn't know 'dead.' She knows 'fish,' and that fish belong to water and that water belongs to fish, and so, for her, this fish is just where it ought to be, doing just what it ought to do. The rocking waves undulate the fish's body to give it some appearance of self-determined movement. The fish lies flat on the water, unlike the fish we'd danced with. But it is in motion, it has moved into shore from some distance out in the water, and it's rocking up and down now in harmony with the waves.

I can tell Dylan, "The fish is dead." But what will that mean to her? Is 'dead' a color? A way of moving? A word that means "there's only one, this time, not a whole, bright school of them"?

Dylan doesn't know 'dead.' She knows only life, not as a contrast to anything, not as the opposite of death, but simply as the way things are. Animated and ever-changing, the Earth reaches toward her and she reaches back. 'Alive' is everything, not circumscribed by any defining parameters. Dylan doesn't have a conceptual understanding of 'dead' because she doesn't have a conceptual understanding of 'alive.'

I lift the tiny silver fish from the water and hold it on the palm of my hand. Dylan and I bend over the fish, studying its sleek body, its unblinking eyes, its v-ing tail, the delicate filigree of its scales. We touch our fingertips to the fish's belly and explore the coolness of its skin and its texture, neither smooth nor rough, but 'bumpy,' as Dylan describes it.

To look so closely at a fish is an unexpected intimacy. Studying this tiny fish in my hand, we see the particularities of the fish that we chased as a shining cluster of motion—we know the school, now, to be made up of these individuals, each muscling from the water in lively leaps, and, so, we know the school more fully. And our play with the school shapes how we see this tiny fish lying on my palm. We know its spirited energy, its flash and spark, its dart and dapple. We look at it through the lens of its dynamic life.

Dylan is learning 'fish'—leaping fish, swimming fish, and, now, this fish gazing up at her. This new-come knowledge of fish is an impossible context for her to learn 'dead.' I do say the words to her: "This fish is not jumping like the other fish because this fish is dead." I don't know what else to say, beyond these few, unintelligible words: how can I explain fish death to a person who knows fish life through only two encounters and as images in books (and those fish—book fish—are always motionless, just like this fish in my hand).

Dylan answers me. "Fish. Water," she says. Dylan knows that fish belong in water, that this fish belongs in the lake. That is the story of fish life, and that is the only story we're in, right now.

I slide the fish into Dylan's hand and she slides the fish into the inch-deep water at the edge of the lake. We watch the waves carry the small silver creature a short distance out into the water, and we watch the fish move along the shoreline as though it were swimming across the surface of the lake.

Months later, on the bright edge of spring, I make a gift of caterpillars to Dylan and her sister. I order them from a science education company. It makes me squirm to buy living creatures from a business, but I override my unease because I want Dylan to experience the birth of a butterfly, and I believe that she, more than anyone I know, has the capacity to be a patient witness to that birth.

The caterpillars arrive tiny and lively, ready to occupy the mesh tent that will be their home as they move from caterpillar to chrysalides to Painted Lady butterflies. We set up the tent, follow the instructions about what sorts of flowers and leaves to put in with the caterpillars and about how to hang the caterpillars' little tub of food, and then, Dylan and her sister, Paden, tip the caterpillars out of their shipping vial and into the tent.

Starting this first day, then, watching the caterpillars becomes our daily meditation. We watch them wrinkle their way across leaves. We watch them lie around. We watch them eat. We watch the tiny black specks of their poop accumulate at the bottom of the tent (this holds particular fascination for Dylan). We watch the caterpillars grow long and thick, as they shed their skin several times over.

And one day, after about a week, we watch the caterpillars hang themselves upside-down from the twigs in the tent. Over the course of the day, each caterpillar's skin hardens into a chrysalis, the shell in which it will reshape itself from a caterpillar to a butterfly.

Now, our watching becomes waiting. The chrysalides hang unmoving, day after day. Reddish-brown, ridged and rough, they look like dead leaves. Dylan seems unconcerned with the waiting; for her, our vigil at the tent is, simply, an obvious continuation of our daily practice of gazing through the mesh at what it holds. For a while, it held caterpillars. Now it holds these quiet structures that I name for her: "Those are chrysalides. The caterpillars are inside them, changing into butterflies." We look into the tent each morning before we leave the house and first thing when we return, and just before Dylan's nap and as soon as she's awake. We keep a close eye on the chrysalides, coming to know them as intimately as we knew the caterpillars that they once were.

And, eventually and miraculously, late one afternoon when we check the mesh tent, we find butterflies. Three of them, new-emerged, stand on leaves at the bottom of the tent. Their wings are still chrysalis-damp, and aren't yet inflated with blood; the butterflies are opening and closing them in a slow-motion echo of flight, shaping their wings into deep-orange velvet triangles striped and spotted with black, brown, and white.

Well, that's what happens for two of the butterflies. The third butterfly tries to inflate its wings; the pulse and muscle of its effort is visible in its small quivering body. One wing is partially open, but bent at an awkward angle; the other wing remains folded and wrinkled.

Two butterflies, wings at a slow flutter. One butterfly, struggling.

Dylan speaks first. "Butterfly?!" she exclaims, linking these new arrivals with the fluttering creatures that she knows well in the backyard.

"Yes, butterflies!" I answer. "These are Painted Lady butterflies. They grew inside the chrysalides. These are the butterflies we've been waiting for!"

"Chrysalis. Caterpillar," Dylan says. I wonder how she understands any of this: caterpillars into chrysalides, chrysalides breaking open, butterflies stepping out into the long-quiet mesh tent. Wings first folded and then unfurled. Butterflies in a tent in the house rather than flying bright through green and sky. Witnessing this miracle of caterpillar-to-butterfly stretches our imagination to its outer edges, it demands a preposterous shift in perspective: How can it be that such delicate, bold color emerges from a dry brown leaf? That earth-bound creatures grow wings and fly? There is science to explain metamorphosis, and metaphors abound to link this transformation to other miracles—rebirth, enlightenment, renewal. But, for now, standing at the mesh tent, Dylan and I have only our wonderment at life, new-made, have only our witness, our held-breath silence and our exclamations.

We linger a long time at the mesh tent, talking together, and quiet together. The bent-winged butterfly especially compels our attention, as it works to unfurl its wings.

"I wonder if the butterfly will get its wings open, like the other ones," I say. I have a vague understanding that there is only a small window of time just after emergence for butterflies' wings to take shape. I worry about the bent-winged butterfly: will its wings become locked into crooked misalignment? What life can a butterfly have, without flight?

Dylan seems not particularly concerned. She meets my worry with a simple affirmation: "Butterfly. Wings." This is how she knows the

135

world to be: butterflies have wings and fly. There is nothing in her experience that gives her reason to anticipate any other outcome for this butterfly: "Butterfly. Wings."

Over the next few days, the strong-winged butterflies fill the mesh tent with lifting, looping flight, while the crumple-winged butterfly walks calmly from twig to bloom to leaf, active though earthbound. One sunny morning, we carry the mesh tent into the backyard and ceremoniously release the two healthy butterflies, sending them out into the great green world. The third butterfly stays in the mesh tent, which confuses Dylan.

"Butterfly flying away?" she asks, gesturing to the crumple-winged butterfly. "Bye-bye butterfly!" This has been Dylan's send-off for the other butterflies: "Flying! Bye-bye!" She's prepared to launch the third butterfly with the same exclamations and farewells.

"Sweetheart, this butterfly can't fly like the others, because of its hurt wing," I explain.

Dylan crouches close to the tent, peering in at the butterfly. Then she says, quietly, "Hurt wing. Crying." And she begins to whimper in a mock cry, an echo of her own tears when she's hurt.

I listen, stunned, to Dylan's improvised, empathetic tears, to her raw, rough voice that sounds just as it does when she cries.

"Butterfly wings," Dylan had said, when this butterfly first emerged. An affirmation: butterflies have wings and fly; this is the way of things. Now, Dylan understands another possibility: injury, and sadness, and no flight. A new way of seeing butterflies, yes, and a new perspective, that of the butterfly, hurt and sorrowful, and crying. From this new perspective, relationship: with this butterfly, Dylan shares the knowledge of tears.

We care for the crumpled-wing butterfly as best we can, in its solitary, tented life. We give it sugar water and fresh camellia blooms, and our pity. But after a few days alone in the tent, the butterfly dies.

We find it on its side on the floor of the tent. It doesn't move, not even when I reach in to touch it in an effort to stir it back to life.

I lift the butterfly from the tent and hold it on my palm. Dylan bends close over the quiet butterfly, touching its soft, crumpled wing with a tentative finger. "Hurt wing," she says.

"Yes, sweetheart, the butterfly had a hurt wing, and couldn't fly," I say. "Now, the butterfly is dead. It's done living."

It's been months since we encountered the dead fish at the lake, and we've not been in the company of death since then. What will Dylan understand of death now, that she didn't understand then?

Only this: that some butterflies move across the sky on strong wings, and that a butterfly with an injured wing cannot fly, and cries. That we take care of that butterfly, tending to its life and well-being.

Only this: that a butterfly with an injured wing walks around its circumscribed home, upright and active—until one day it stops walking, and lies toppled onto its good wing, unmoving.

Only this, spoken simply and truly by Dylan, gazing at the butter-fly on my hand: "Butterfly all done. Hurt wing. All done crying."

Seeing with New Eyes

How to paint with perspective: "Imagine the picture surface as an open window through which to see the painted world," instructs the website for the Boston Museum of Science. Then, create a horizon line, with a vanishing point where the visual rays of sight come together.

Could this also be instruction for how to live in the world— for how to cultivate an ability to see from new vantage-points? Look at the world as if through an open window, with a horizon that beckons. Gaze at that horizon seeking to see what lies there, and, as you gaze, allow your previous perspectives to vanish until there is only the new-seen world opening before you.

The origins of the word 'perspective' are rooted in medieval Latin: *perspectivus*, meaning 'sight,' 'look through,' 'inspect.' To see clearly, to see anew, to see. When we change perspective—when we step away from our habitual ways of seeing and understanding—we find new details in familiar landscapes, we discover connections in what had seemed unrelated, we re-contextualize the long-known. When we change perspective, the horizon line shifts, stale assumptions vanish, new possibilities are revealed.

Spring wrestles its way to the surface through long stretches of wet and gray, and the rain seems near-constant. Everywhere that Dylan and I walk, we encounter rain puddles. Which is, for Dylan, a great delight. She is crazy for rain puddles. She strides through them giddy in her rubber, knee-high, red-and-black 'ladybug boots'—strides, runs, jumps, laughs. Some days, we spend the whole morning in rain puddles. Other days, rain puddles are stepping stones that carry us forward to our destination.

Dylan splashes through spring in her ladybug boots, right to the bright edge of summer. And then, the rain eases and the puddles dry, and the boots come off, and Dylan comes to know 'sandals'— and even better, bare feet. "Beach feet," Dylan calls them. 'Beach feet' become Dylan's passion: beach feet in the grass, beach feet on the gravel-and-dirt bike trail, beach feet on the sidewalk, beach feet at the beach. When we arrive someplace—anyplace— she pleads to take her sandals off. And once they're off, she wants to keep them off, emphatically resisting my requests to slip her sandals back on to cross a parking lot, or enter the library, or go to the grocery store.

On a warm day in early June, Dylan and I visit the Arboretum, abundant with bloom and bold green. There are sprinklers showering the grassy meadow there—and puddling the unpaved path through the green field.

"Rain puddle!" Dylan cries out, running to the edge of a mud-brown puddle. "Ladybug boots?" She looks at her sandaled feet, and at me, and at the puddle. "Ladybug boots, please." Her intention is clear: she aims to wade into the puddle, and is hesitating only long enough for me to produce the suddenly necessary ladybug boots.

"Dylan," I say. "This puddle is from a sprinkler. It's a sprinkler puddle. You can—" Dylan interrupts me. "Ladybug boots in rain puddle. Please."

I'm moved by her determination, and by the story she's telling with her eager request, the story of rain puddles, in which boots play a leading role—the only story of puddles that Dylan knows.

"Dylan, you wear your ladybug boots in rain puddles when the weather is chilly. Your boots keep your feet warm. But today, the air and sun will keep you warm. On a summer day like today, you can run through sprinkler puddles with bare feet—with beach feet."

Dylan looks at me, hopeful and uncertain: "Puddle beach feet?"

"Yes, sweetheart. Beach feet in the puddle," I confirm.
"Can I help you take off your sandals?"

My offer is unnecessary. Dylan's already tugging at the straps, pulling her sandals off and tossing them aside. She strides to the puddle's edge, grins at me, and steps into it. She crosses the shallow water, and then turns and races back through it. Back and forth through the puddle, and again, and again, she runs, laughing, jumping, splashing.

The story of rain puddles and the story of bare feet have been, for Dylan, two different stories, unrelated. Today, those stories change, become two ways of telling a larger story, the story of feet-in-water, sometimes booted, sometimes bare.

And then, the story expands. Dylan looks up the path to the next puddle, and freezes. There is a dog running through that puddle.

"Dog beach feet?" Dylan murmurs, trying out an idea. "Dog beach feet in puddle?"

It is a moment of revelation for Dylan: dogs have bare feet!

I am astonished by her astonishment. I've assumed that she knows that dogs have bare feet—or, actually, I've not even thought about what Dylan perceives or doesn't perceive about dogs' feet. Of course dogs have bare feet, it's part of the definition of dog; I'd never considered this to be something to point out to Dylan, a particular angle to highlight in her growing acquaintance with dogs. I don't know what Dylan has thought about dogs' feet, not until this moment, when she stands barefoot in a puddle and sees a dog barefoot in a puddle.

"Dog beach feet." And then, a bold intellectual leap. Gesturing to a nearby crow, Dylan asks, "Crow beach feet?"

"Yes, Dylan, yes! The dog has bare feet, and the crow has bare feet." I'm not sure what else to say, what other affirmation or information would be helpful. I'm still making my own sense of Dylan's new perspective, which has startled me into a new way of looking at the dog.

"Crow beach feet," Dylan says with more sureness. "Dog beach feet."

Then, another leap: "Robin beach feet?" There's no robin in sight. "Chickadee beach feet?" No chickadee here, either.

Dylan doesn't need them to be here. She's calling to mind the creatures that are familiar and dear to her, creatures that she sees, now, with fresh eyes: barefooted, like her.

When we look from a new perspective, the horizon shifts. The world changes.

We can look and look at a thing until it becomes familiar and dear, and we think that we know it—and, then, a change in perspective offers a new context or story, illuminates a detail, illustrates a pattern. We see the thing fresh, with more complexity and nuance.

This shift in understanding both requires and strengthens in us the qualities of imagination and curiosity, the willingness to reconsider what we'd thought to be true, to re-examine our assumptions, to see connections. We think by analogy, we speak in metaphor— which corresponds to "an investigative attitude toward reality, to participation that allows our thoughts to open out," writes Vea Vecchi. Shifting perspective as an act of participation in the world, yes! We don't look through the window—the instructions for how to paint with perspective have it wrong. We step through the window, like Alice into Wonderland, and marvel at what we find: barefoot dogs and crows, warm-water puddles on clear-sky days.

How do we make these shifts in perspective that open us into the world's mysteries and marvels? How do we experience both familiarity and novelty? How do we find the surprise waiting in the details that we know well? These questions shaped my days with Dylan.

To answer those questions, I sought opportunities for us to linger in texture and fragrance, melody and pulse, line and shape and tang. One day, we spent a full morning with a maple tree. We sat under it with our backs against its fine-ridged bark. We lay down so we could see the undersides of its leaves, and its limbs branching and twigs reaching, and the sky overarching. We put our tongues to the amber drop of sap where a branch had broken away. We put our cheeks to the bark. We crumpled a leaf fallen from the tree, and split open the helicoptering seed pods to look inside. We took a handful of the seed pods to the highest place we could find nearby and tossed them into the air. We watched a leaf fall. We closed our eyes and listened to a leaf fall.

As I worked to strengthen our ability to look at things from unfamiliar points of view in order to refresh our relationships with them, I remembered what I'd learned from The Private Eye Project, a course of study using jewelers' loupes as a tool for seeing from new perspectives. The Private Eye Project coaches participants to think by analogy, harnessing curiosity and imagination to ask: "What does this remind me of? Why?" Analogy invites us to look through the lens of relationship to see the identity of a thing more clearly. Our experience and knowledge of one thing inform how we come to know another thing. This re-aligning of knowledge and experience opens into stories and hypotheses, into revelation and renewal. The Private Eye Project describes analogy as "the main tool of the scientist, poet, visual artist, inventor, humorist, teacher, preacher"—people whose work is intellectual and soulful, and concerned with what we know, and what we feel, and how we behave. This is the broad reach of analogy.

"By means of analogy," writes philosopher Kathleen Dean Moore, "We visualize what is too large or too small to be seen. . . . [We] move ourselves to understand and sometimes to love what we have never before imagined."

> *A small silver chime hangs at the doorway to Dylan's house. Each day, when we leave the house and when we arrive home, I lift Dylan to the chime and she rings it. "Chime," I say to her. "Chime," she echoes.*
>
> *One day in the early spring when catkins lengthen on the birch and alder trees in the neighborhood, I lift Dylan to an alder branch so she can touch the tree's dangling tassels. Dylan flips the catkins with the same gesture that she uses to ring the chimes at the threshold of her home—and then is quiet, expectant, listening. "Chimes?" she asks.*
>
> *Startled and delighted, I say, "Oh—actually, these are catkins."*
>
> *"Catkins," Dylan repeats. She flips and tips the catkins, laughing, calling out "Catkins!"*
>
> *When we return home that morning, I lift Dylan to the chimes at the front door, as I always do. Dylan tips and flips them, and, laughing, exclaims, "Catkins!"*

Listening by analogy, thinking by analogy: *How is a catkin like a chime?* This question can carry us through the window into wonderland. . . .

Analogy stirs not only our minds, but our hearts. *How is a catkin like a worm?*

> *Walking in the neighborhood, we come to a patch of sidewalk scattered with a half-dozen catkins fallen from a birch tree. When she spies the catkins, Dylan calls out, "Worms!" She squats over them, just as she squats over worms splayed on the sidewalk after rain. She picks up one of the catkins, lays it on her palm, and carries it to the soil under the birch tree, tipping it gently down on the damp earth. "Dirt. Worm. Safe." This is just what we do when we find worms in distress on the sidewalk: we carry them back to earth.*
>
> *One by one, Dylan moves the catkins to the soil, practicing worm rescue.*

When is a catkin like a worm? When it needs our help, like a worm after rain.

Dylan made such leaps of perception all the time: chime-catkin, catkin-worm. She was alert to details because so much that she encountered was new to her, and unfamiliar. She gathered the details of a thing in order to know it: *What is this thing? Have I seen anything like it before?*

I could glance at something and assume that I knew what it was because I'd seen it many times before: a chime was a chime, a catkin was a catkin, a worm was a worm, their lives and characters occupied different contexts. It was a startle when Dylan linked disparate things—and refreshing, and delighting, and enlivening.

With Dylan, I began to pay attention to details that helped me see things fresh. I curled my hand to make a narrow lens for looking close. I bent low, I lay on my belly. I looked from below, I lay on my back. I challenged myself to look at something for five seconds, consciously counting 1-2-3-4-5. That was a long gaze, a contrast to my habitual quick-glancing looks. I stretched the count: eight seconds, ten seconds.

With Dylan, I asked the questions, out loud and often: *What does this remind me of? Have I seen anything like this before?* I trained my mind to analogy, adopting the "investigative attitude toward reality" that Vecchi describes, wanting my thoughts to open out in the way that Dylan's so instinctively did.

An ecological identity is anchored by dispositions to pay attention, to be curious, to open our hearts. Which is to say: an ecological identity is anchored by empathy.

What is it to be a worm? It is a complex life, Dylan and I learned:

> *A worm on the sidewalk after rain is frantic, unmoored from the moist dark soil, desperately flipping and flinging itself toward safety.*

> *A worm dangling from a robin's beak is lunch — unless the robin drops it because a dog races toward it, which is, for the worm, salvation, but which is, for the robin, a loss and continued hunger.*

146

A worm carefully carried from the garden to the family room is a caring offering made to a newt during its brief caged residency at home—a sacrifice made on behalf of another being.

A hundred worms carried in a cardboard tub from the garden shop are riches for the backyard pea patch when they are tucked gently into the new-tilled soil.

What is it to know a worm? Concern for its flailing fear, and quick protectiveness. Dismay when it is in danger, sorrow when it is wounded, consternation when we willingly send it to its death. Unqualified gladness when it burrows into a nourishing home that will, in turn, nourish the bounty of peas that we hope to grow.

Empathy: the awareness of another being's feelings; the ability to take up another being's point of view. We nurture empathy when we practice seeing the world from new and unfamiliar perspectives. Looking through a window, not into a mirror, we see from another being's point of view, we imaginatively enter into another being's experience, we feel the pulse and throb of another being's heart.

Empathy is cornerstone in an ecological identity. Empathy turns us toward the living world with imagination and curiosity, with courage enough to let go of our habitual and easy understandings, with willingness to experience the vulnerability of disequilibrium. Empathy sizes us in right proportion to others, not more-than, or better-than, or worthier-than, but connected by the shared capacity for joy and suffering.

Empathy asks that we consider the well-being of other creatures when we act. The etymology of 'empathy' is instructive; it comes from the Greek *empatheia*: "affection, passion, partiality." Empathy braided into an ecological identity asks that we act with partiality for the Earth and its beyond-human beings—with partiality for the worm on the sidewalk.

Look through the open window at the great wide world.
Mark a point on the horizon and start walking toward it.
Leave your well-worn perspectives at the windowsill as you cross over into the familiar world seen anew. "It's a paltry sense of wonder that requires something new every day," writes Kathleen Dean Moore. "To be worthy of the astonishing world, a sense of wonder will be a way of life, in every place and time, no matter how familiar."

References

Kathleen Dean Moore. *Wild Comfort: The Solace of Nature*.
Boston: Trumpeter, 2010.

Kathleen Dean Moore. "The Journey of the Universe:
Metaphors of Music and Life." Presentation at the
Yale Conference on the Journey of the Universe, March 2011.

Kerry Ruef. *The Private Eye: (5X) Looking/Thinking by Analogy*.
Seattle: The Private Eye Project, 2003.

Vea Vecchi. *Art and Creativity in Reggio Emilia*.
New York: Routledge, 2010.

Create Stories

Eat Like Heron

Dylan and I have just come to shore from our first paddle on Lake Washington in a kayak. We've hauled the boat onto a dock at a paddle club, stripped off our life jackets, and put on our shoes. I'm reluctant to leave the lake, though it's nearly time for lunch and for Dylan's nap; we've had a grand morning on the water, and I want to savor it a little longer. So I suggest to Dylan that we walk along the urban shoreline to look at the boats and the marine shops that line the lake, and Dylan says, "Yes, yes, a walk!" And so we leave the paddle club and amble along the waterfront.

We follow a rough shoreline footpath past a marina with boats moored along a gated dock and toward a row of weathered houseboats. Tucked between the two docks is a ragged wetland, cordoned off from the footpath by black site fencing that encloses a few pluming bunches of landscaped grasses and one frail sapling staked with rubber tubing to a metal post. The air has the heady smell of gas and moist fertile earth. Here, in this grubby, closed-in wetland, a heron stands in the shallows.

When I see it, I stop walking and kneel close to Dylan. "Great blue heron," I whisper to her. This is her first encounter with these birds that stand as tall as her, all sharp angles and jagged feathers. "Great blue heron," she whispers back, tangling the syllables but capturing the reverence she hears in my voice. I sit on the footpath, Dylan lowers herself onto my lap, and we watch the heron.

Long, quiet minutes pass. The heron, motionless: body poised, head angled toward the water, eyes intent, unblinking. Dylan and I, silent echoes of the heron's stillness. We watch the heron and the heron watches for fish, all of us with a singleness of attention and commitment that binds us to the moment and to each other.

Then stillness breaks open. The heron plunges its bill into the water.

Dylan and I startle. Before we've fully registered the fast lunge, the heron stands tall again, a fish dangling from its long sword of a bill. "Fish," exhales Dylan.

The heron gives several quick jerks of its head to re-position the fish, and then opens its bill and tilts the fish in. It pulls its long, thin neck tight against its body, flattening the graceful curve as it works the fish down its throat. After a visible gulping swallow, the heron straightens, returning to its unmoving watchfulness.

Dylan looks at me, eyes wide. I hesitate before speaking, wary of clouding this moment. Wanting to give Dylan language for what she's witnessed. Wanting her witnessing to remain bigger than words. I keep it simple: "The heron caught a fish to eat. The fish is the heron's food."

Dylan listens, gazing at the heron standing quiet in the shallows. Then she tries out the idea I've offered: "Heron eat a fish?" I nod, and in a moment Dylan stirs in my lap, ready to move on. We leave the heron and follow the footpath home for lunch.

For lunch: chunks of cantaloupe, roasted beets, steamed carrots cut into bite-sized rounds. Dylan climbs into her highchair and stills herself. There is an electric quiet to her body, a fierce attentiveness that compels my attention. Dylan begins to move her eyes slowly side to side, grazing them over the food on the highchair's tray. Then: a lunge forward, and quickly upright again, cantaloupe held in teeth. Dylan gives the cantaloupe three quick jerks, then tilts her head back and swallows. And returns to her wild, watchful posture. Eyes riveted on the food that awaits her capture, she whispers, "I eat like heron."

Telling a Good Story

The wild requires that we learn the terrain, nod to all the plants and animals and birds, ford the streams and cross the tides, and tell a good story when we get home.

Gary Snyder, "The Etiquette of Freedom" in *The Practice of the Wild*

"*Once upon a time*," says the storyteller—and we lean close, anticipating adventure, anticipating emotion and insight, calamity and revelation—anticipating a story. We give over our imaginations, readying ourselves for new landscapes, for characters who will become real to us, whose feelings and fate will matter. We fall into the rhythm and lilt of language. We step out of our forward-moving lives to linger in the life of a story.

Stories are elemental and essential for us humans. We tell stories to find our place in this astonishing world, to affirm order and meaning in the tumble of life, to imagine new possibilities and to offer moral contours for our behavior. Stories "gather experience into shapes we can hold and pass on," says Scott Russell Sanders. And Terry Tempest Williams says that stories remind us "what it means to be human, living in place with our neighbors." John Tallmadge writes that stories "make relationships visible and tangible so that they can be remembered, studied, understood, shared, and preserved." Though entertaining, stories are not entertainment; they are fundamental to how we engage our lives, our communities, our home terrain.

Dylan taught me that.

Dylan's first language was story. During our year together, she was just coming into spoken English. And she used her blossoming knowledge of speech to tell stories. Eloquent, one-word stories, at first: "Crow." "Apple." "Rock." These stories, animated with gesture and expression and tone, described important happenings. They contained humor and tenderness, delight and curiosity. They held lively action and referenced a full cast of characters. They spoke of the places we'd been, the creatures we'd seen, the ways in which we'd participated in the play of water and sand, shadow and light, in the unfurling, beckoning world.

Well—that's mostly true. Dylan's stories became stories in the intersection of her telling and my listening. With her stories, Dylan said "Remember?" In the ancient and honored way of storytelling, she evoked our shared experiences and infused them with memory and imagination and relevance. "Crow," she said, and, listening, I understood the story inside the word, because I'd been there with her when it unfolded. The story went like this: "Once upon a time, just this morning, we heard a crow crying its crow-calls loud and harsh. It was on the telephone wire overhead, swaying with the movement of the line. We watched it until it launched itself into flight and, still crying out, threaded its way through the tree-tips and out of sight." Dylan's stories confirmed our experiences together, and, in that confirmation, reconnected us to those experiences and to each other.

"Robin!" Dylan exclaims, stopping abruptly in her meander down the sidewalk. A robin stands a few feet ahead of her, at the border where grass meets sidewalk; when Dylan spots the bird, it has just plucked a worm from the grass.

The worm dangles for a moment from the robin's beak, then, with a quick toss of its head, the robin swallows it.

"Worm! Robin!" Dylan exclaims. She shakes her head in a gesture that mimics the robin's quick-tilted head as it swallowed the worm.

The robin plucks another worm from the damp grass, but something invisible to us startles the bird, and it drops the worm on the sidewalk and flies swiftly away. "Worm!" Dylan cries out, rushing to the writhing creature on the sidewalk. Dylan seems both compelled by the worm and uncertain how to engage it; she squats close and looks intently, but doesn't reach to touch it, and startles back when it flips toward her.

Unsure if Dylan has seen a bird eat a worm before, I describe what we'd witnessed: "The robin plucked a worm from the dirt with its beak and swallowed it. Then, the robin picked up another worm to eat. But something startled the robin, and it dropped the worm and flew away."

"Robin. Worm. Beak. Flying. Worm sidewalk," Dylan says, retelling the dramatic and unnerving story.

"The robin pulled the worm out of the soil, where it lives. Shall we put the worm back?" I ask.

"Ann do it!" Dylan commands.

I lift the worm onto my palm and hold out my hand so that Dylan can take a last look at the worm. Then, I set the worm in the sliver of moist earth at the edge of the lawn. Dylan bends over the worm, watching it wriggle into the soil; even after it's out of sight, she lingers, studying the earth. "Robin. Beak. Worm. Dirt. Home." she says, telling the story of this patch of sidewalk where a robin hunted worms, the story of a worm that fell from danger into our provenance, the story of a simple kind gesture.

Compelling action, strong emotion: the robin, the worm, the release, the rescue. Action and emotion revisited in the storytelling.

In his essay, "The Power of Stories," Scott Russell Sanders makes a list of ten reasons for telling and hearing stories. Here's his list:

> *Stories entertain us. They create community. They help us see through the eyes of others. They show us the consequences of our actions. They educate our desires. Stories help us dwell in place. They help us dwell in time. They help us deal with suffering, loss, and death. They teach us how to be human. And stories acknowledge the wonder and mystery of Creation.*

Robin. Worm. Beak. Dirt. Worm. Home: Dylan's six-word story nails everything on Sanders' list.

I wrestled with how much to talk to Dylan. I am given to words, to talk-talk-talking about things. I am seduced by language and compelled by story. I relish the sweet intimacy in nestling close and telling stories. I could have swathed Dylan in words.

But, oh, I did not want my words to suffocate Dylan's own meaning-making, did not want my words to come between

Dylan's experiences of the world and her inward embrace of those experiences. I did not want to turn our encounters into natural history lessons or literacy drills, all about names and nouns, action words and descriptors. I did not want to circumscribe experience, but, rather, to expand and illuminate it. And so I hesitated to speak, weighing my words carefully, offering them sparingly.

Not Dylan, though—there was no hesitation in her speech! She sought out language with which she could describe her experiences. She used story to affirm her witness of and participation in the wide natural world. With her stories, Dylan wove us into the community of people who marvel together at the beyond-human world.

And, so, Dylan and I developed a rhythm of storytelling that included both silence and language. Out in the world, I aimed to speak with a light touch, offering explanations of what we encountered without much editorial commentary, leaving space in which the experiences could ring with their own resonance. And Dylan seized the language I offered and wove it together with gesture and expression and tone to create evocative stories. We became storytellers together, Dylan and I.

As Dylan's knowledge of language grew, her stories expanded from one word to simple phrases and sentences: a few words could hold a whole morning's adventure. Between Dylan's expanding vocabulary and my deliberate nudging, our stories began to reference emotion and mood, questions and musings: "I wonder how the worm felt when it lay on the sidewalk." "Worm wiggling. Worm sad. Worm go home."

We used field-guides as storybooks. The field guide's illustrations of familiar birds, flowers, shells, and mammals sparked reminiscences: "Crow! Wire, moving like this." "Butterfly. Hurt wing. All done."

We began to make up stories starring the creatures and places we'd seen: "I wonder where the robin went, when it dropped the worm and flew away." "I wonder what the worm's home is like, inside the earth." And we began to tell each other stories of experiences that we'd had when we were apart: "Last night, I heard a creature skittering in the bushes outside my bedroom window. When I looked out to see what it was—I saw a rat!" "Park with mommy. Dog catch frisbee!"

To what point, all this storytelling? Why did it matter?

Our stories tethered us to the places we frequented and to the creatures we encountered. They made our witness of the beyond-human world tangible by giving it words and substance, carried our witness deeply into our consciousness, and strengthened our capacity for empathy. Our stories allowed us to see the land more fully, through the overlaid lenses of memory and history, imagination and knowledge. The land became more dynamic and lively, more textured and nuanced, more *known*, because we engaged the land through stories. We knew the land better because we told stories about it. Stories bind us to place.

Stories also bind us to each other. Many of the stories that Dylan and I exchanged had particular resonance because we'd been companions when the stories were born; the stories were ways of saying, "We witnessed that together; we share this knowledge of the world." And the stories that Dylan and I exchanged about experiences we'd had when we were apart opened our lives to each other, deepened the ways in which we knew each other and what we each cared about. And, so, our stories of place and adventure became stories of relationship.

Stories of relationship, yes—but not only the relationship between storyteller and listener. The stories that Dylan and I told invited us to take the perspectives of other creatures—the frightened worm on the sidewalk, and the hungry robin startled away from its meal. When we look at the world through the eyes of another being, the distinctions between us soften, and the world becomes a more intimate place, its creatures our kin.

Our stories included mention of how we behaved toward the creatures and places we encountered: "Dirt. Worm. Home." Were we generous? Cautious? Playful? Compassionate? Fearful? Stories memorialized our actions, and, in doing so, held us accountable for them.

Our stories offered containers for emotion—delight, fear, sadness, uncertainty. They bookmarked discoveries and opened into questions. Our stories invited us to be more fully human— full-hearted, and thoughtful, curious, eager to understand, awake in mind and spirit.

Stories of place cultivate an ecological identity.

Unlike instructional texts and informational pamphlets, stories about the beyond-human world braid together imagination, emotion, experience, knowledge, and ethics—all elements of an ecological identity. Nuanced and complex, stories engage our hearts as well as our minds, they invite our participation—as storyteller, as listener—in a place. Stories both consolidate and expand how we know a place and its creatures: they locate us within the ecology of a place.

Storytelling begins in observation, unfolds into language, and opens, finally, as an offering, an outward gesture anchored by the inwardness of experience. Storytelling invites us to witness the world's fierce and tender beauty, and renews our astonished and glad participation in the world of herons, of fish daggered and swallowed, of worms on the sidewalk, of crows on telephone wires.

References

Scott Russell Sanders, "The Power of Stories" in
The Force of the Spirit. Boston: Beacon Press, 2000.

Gary Snyder, "The Etiquette of Freedom" in
The Practice of the Wild. San Francisco: North Point Press, 1990.

John Tallmadge. "Linked through story: Natural science,
nature writing, and traditional ecological knowledge."
Journal of Natural History Education and Experience, 5:49-57, 2011.

Terry Tempest Williams, "Home Work," in
Red: Passion and Patience in the Desert. New York: Pantheon, 2001.

Make Rituals

Pooh Sticks

We visit Ravenna Park for the first time in early October, as the deep, encompassing green of the wooded park begins to rainbow into autumn's red, orange, brown, and yellow. Dylan and I arrive at the park by bus; I tell her that we're going to "the forest and the stream," which is how I want Dylan to know this park— not by its climbers and swing sets, its wading pool and picnic shelter, but by its trees and the sweet flowing stream that's recently been daylighted after too many urban years encased in underground culverts.

The cedar, maple, and alder trees that make up 'the forest' are bedded in a ravine. The trees overarch the small stream that courses along the ravine's floor, and rise above a foot path that winds among them. Dylan and I find our way to the foot path, and follow its meander. We can see Ravenna Creek below us, in its curving bed that runs several feet lower than the path; Dylan stops frequently to peer down at it, commenting on the water's flow and song. Once, she digs a few stones from the dirt of the foot path and throws them hard down-slope toward the stream, but the stones fall short of the water. The stream is tantalizingly close and maddeningly out of reach—until we arrive at a low footbridge that holds us just inches above the water.

That low-lying bridge is exactly what we've needed. Perched on its worn boards, we can, at last, play with the stream.

Leaves have fallen onto the bridge from the big leaf maple at its far side; as Dylan and I squat on the bridge to watch the water's flow, I toss one of the leaves into the stream. The leaf floats. Dylan laughs as we watch it move downstream, spinning and tumbling.

She picks up a leaf from the bridge, holds it over the stream, and drops it into the water. "Leaf! Water!" she exclaims, gesturing to the leaf-in-motion on the water-in-motion.

I gesture, too. "The leaf floats on the water," I say, "And the water carries the leaf."

"Rock splash!" Dylan describes.

I'd not thought of splash, or its absence, when I tossed the leaf into the water—but Dylan, experienced in throwing stones into water, surely had. Expecting a splash, she got, instead, flotation, and the leaf's twirling movement on the water's surface, a new way to know water.

We send more leaves downstream, watching them until they pass under a low overhang of salal and salmonberry branches, and around a curve, and out of sight. Each floating, spinning leaf traces the flow of the stream, gives us a way to read the water's forward movement, to measure its tempo and to track its lift, its turn and tumble.

At some point, we turn to the other side of the bridge, the upstream side. Dylan tosses a leaf into the water from that new stance—and the leaf floats under the bridge and disappears. Dylan, bemused, stares at the stream for a few long moments. Then, she tosses another leaf into the stream—and that leaf, like the one before it, is immediately gone.

Watching Dylan's puzzled study of the stream, I wonder if she's expecting the leaf to flow upstream—or, anyway, to float along the visible length of the stream, as it does on the downstream side.

I realize, with sudden understanding, that Dylan doesn't know 'downstream' and 'upstream'—how could she, at fifteen months old? Unaware that a stream has a uni-directional flow, she doesn't know where to look for the leaf from this side of the bridge.

I decide to show Dylan 'downstream.'

"Dylan, try it again," I encourage her. "Put another leaf in the stream—and I'll show you where it goes."

"Okay," she says, obliging, and drops a leaf into the stream. As it is carried out of sight under the bridge, I take Dylan's hand and hurry with her across the bridge to the downstream side. "Dylan, look! Here comes the leaf! It floated under the bridge." I gesture to the stream, where the leaf is emerging from under our feet.

"Leaf!" Dylan cries out.

"Yes, sweetheart, yes! The stream carried the leaf under the bridge. We couldn't see the leaf when it was under the bridge, but now we can. Look! It's floating down the stream like the other leaves."

"Bridge. Leaf. Stream."

And with this new awareness of water's one-way flow, a game is born.

Dylan crosses to the upstream side of the bridge in two quick strides, tosses a leaf into the water, then hurries to the downstream side, where she squats low on the wood planks to watch the leaf emerge, spin, and float away downstream. She laughs and claps, and calls out, "Leaf! Leaf!" She moves back across the bridge, tosses another leaf into the creek, scurries across the planks to watch it reappear. . . . Back and forth, leaf after leaf, disappearance and return, loss and renewal: Dylan has discovered a watery game of peek-a-boo.

I know the name for this game. I learned it in my grandmother's lap as she read me to sleep: "Pooh Sticks," played by Winnie the Pooh and Piglet, tossing sticks into a stream. Pooh Sticks, played by Dylan and me, tossing leaves from a bridge. Pooh Sticks, a ritual begun on this autumn day that will carry us through the seasons ahead.

For the rest of our year together, each time we visit Ravenna Park, we play Pooh Sticks; it's the first thing we do when we arrive. This simple game serves as a rite of entrance into the park. It is a ritual that says, "We are here, in this place that has held discovery and delight for us; we hope that it will, again, today." A ritual that says, "We are consciously present, attentive to this place, open to what it offers." This is what ritual does: it reminds us that discovery and illuminating leaps of understanding wait for us in each encounter with this lively, ever-unfolding world. Leaves fall. Water flows. Leaves float.

Gestures of Hope and Gratitude

We are shaped by ritual.

Rituals mark the passages that spin our lives forward: birthdays, weddings, funerals, graduation, retirement; we come together in community to honor each other and to recognize life's unfolding. Religious rites and sacraments ritualize encounters with the sacred, and cultivate hope for further holy visitations. Simpler rituals celebrate the daily goodness and generosity of our lives: we say grace, we raise toasts, we kiss each other goodnight.

Ritual lifts us out of the mundane and habitual, and calls our attention to what matters to us. It reminds us of what we hope for and who we hope to be. It binds us to each other and honors the bonds between us. "Ritual," writes storyteller Laura Simms, "confirms our deepest human values: the presence of shared mystery; the magic of language; . . . inspiration for growth; awareness of death and the continuity of life."

What *is* a ritual? "A system of rites," says *Webster's*, "a formal and customarily repeated act or series of acts." Repeated, yes, and with full attention; neither unthinking nor swallowed by habit, ritual that is alive and enlivening is deliberate, anchored by intention and desire. It follows a rhythm and sequence—a litany of words or a series of gestures intended to kindle attentiveness, to awaken memory, to invoke possibility, to renew connection. We often associate the word 'ritual' with religious or spiritual practices, but ritual is more wide-ranging than that: a family ritualizes its life together in the ways that it gathers for meals, or moves toward bedtime, or makes weekend mornings at home. Ritual encompasses both the vitality of whole-hearted expression and the

sweet familiarity of custom. It is formal in its organization—
you can rest into ritual because you know what to expect—but
it is not necessarily stylized or elaborate, nor sober and inward.

*Each time Dylan and I leave her house, we ring the chime that
hangs on the front porch. That simple gesture is an eloquent
avowal: "We are stepping into the great cavalcading world of
crows and rain, blackberry brambles and worms on the sidewalk,
ready to embrace what that world offers us today."*

*At the street corner nearest Dylan's house, a tall smokebush
grows, purple and shimmery. Raindrops catch on its round leaves
and slight branches, beading them with crystals. Each rainy day
that we pass the smokebush, we stop to lift a few raindrops onto
our fingertips, moving with delicate precision. Then—replacing
delicacy with broad movement and laughter—we give the
branches a strong shake, spraying the raindrops into a bright
shower of diamonds. Our rainy day smokebush ritual affirms
that we can meet the rain with attentive gladness.*

*At naptime each afternoon, Dylan and I sing a simple song in
which we embed the names of people dear in her life. Then, we
stand at her bedroom window and look out, to say goodnight to
the creatures and happenings from our morning out in the world:*

Ann: *Goodnight, Lake Washington.*
Dylan: *Goodnight, toes in the water.*
Ann: *Goodnight, mallards in the water.*

Dylan: *Goodnight, rock splash in the water.*
Ann: *Goodnight, bare-foot Dylan.*
Dylan: *Goodnight, bare-foot Ann.*

Simple, repeated acts, these rituals. They kept us awake to the
world and to our movement through it. They called our attention
to what we might otherwise not have noticed. These rituals
reminded us to participate with gladness in the unfolding life
of the world, making our lives with intention and awareness,
and with no small joy.

I ought to acknowledge, here, that I am pre-disposed to ritual.
I grew up in the Catholic Church; my mom worked as a pastoral
associate for several parishes, coordinating religious education
and lay ministry. As a child, I spent plenty of time at church,
in a spiritual tradition steeped in ritual. And so I am partial to
the symbolic and graceful gestures of ritual both grand and quiet.

But during my year with Dylan, my understanding of ritual —
both what it looks like and what it signifies — shifted. I'd known
ritual to be formal and facilitated: Sunday Mass, or high holy
days like Easter. I'd also experienced the potency of personal
ritual, inward and anchoring: a daily morning journal; birthday
candles lit at sunrise, and intentions set for the year ahead.
With Dylan, I learned that rituals can also be organic upwellings,
not so much planned or even intended, but moments seized
and carried forward, significant both in their initial experience
and in their resonant repetition as ritual. I didn't set out to
Make a Ritual of ringing the chimes each time we left the
house or of playing with the rain on the neighbor's smokebush.

But once we'd rung the chimes a few times, once we'd stopped
at the smokebush for several rainy days in a row, it seemed
right to carry on, to formalize these experiences into ritual
gestures of attention and participation—that is, as long as
they remained true-hearted expressions, sources of gladness and
connection.

With Dylan, I learned that, when a ritual becomes stale, or forced,
or pro forma—an echo rather than a song—it is no longer useful,
and best allowed to fall away, in the trust that another moment will
offer itself with all the resonance of ritual. There came a morning
when our stop at the smokebush felt hollow: we gave a shake of
the rain-dropped leaves as we always had, but I felt impatient,
suddenly bored with the bush and the oft-repeated play with the
rain on its leaves. Dylan, too, seemed indifferent, going through
the motions half-heartedly. The ritual had lost its liveliness
and there was no point in carrying on with it. We revisited the
smokebush every so often during the months that followed,
remembering with smiling stories how we'd played with the rain
that collected on its leaves—but that play was no longer an active
and regular part of our movement through the neighborhood.

What else did I learn about ritual, during my year with Dylan?
That ritual is a way to call forward what matters to us.
Dylan and I created rituals to link us to places that we
visited often and cared about, rituals that reminded us that
"this place has held us well. We are coming to know its contours
and character. It has been significant to us, and will continue to
be. It will open further for us, and we will embrace it further."
The ritual of Pooh Sticks at Ravenna Park honored knowledge
of water's coursing flow downstream, honored the discovery
that comes from disorientation and from sudden shifts in

perspective, honored marvel and delight. The ritual of saying goodnight to the cast of characters from each day's outing honored the relationships that can take root when we participate in the life of a place, and honored the possibility of relationships still to come, encounters yet to happen.

That speaks to another thing I learned about ritual. We create rituals to remind us of how we hope to behave. Playing with raindrops on the smokebush reminded Dylan and me to dance with the rain rather than resentfully hunching up our shoulders against its frequent, damp company. Ringing the chime as we left the house created a threshold moment of crossing from home into the wide, pulsing world, and, at that threshold, reminded us to pay attention to what might offer itself during the morning, to be alert for opportunities to join ourselves to the world we would encounter.

These are the ways that ritual nurtures an ecological identity. An ecological identity is rooted in care for and knowledge of the beyond-human world, and a commitment to live in honorable relationship with that world and with the other beings who share it with us. These are qualities that ritual affirms and strengthens. Ritual cultivates the practice of deliberately honoring beauty and delight and discovery, astonishment and reverence. Ritual hones our attention and lively awareness, and calls forward who we want to be and how we want to live in a place. Ritual celebrates the places that matter to us, and the creatures who reside there, and the experiences that we have there. Ritual links us to other people who live with us in a place. Ritual, then, becomes formative in the development of an ecological identity in young children— and in ourselves.

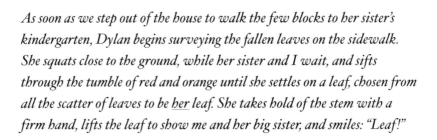

As soon as we step out of the house to walk the few blocks to her sister's kindergarten, Dylan begins surveying the fallen leaves on the sidewalk. She squats close to the ground, while her sister and I wait, and sifts through the tumble of red and orange until she settles on a leaf, chosen from all the scatter of leaves to be <u>her</u> leaf. She takes hold of the stem with a firm hand, lifts the leaf to show me and her big sister, and smiles: "Leaf!"

<u>Now</u> we can walk to school. I bundle Dylan into the baby carrier on my chest, where she holds tight to the leaf as we chat and walk to the elementary school. The school is on the far side of a well-trafficked street, and fifth graders serve as crossing guards, escorting arriving students and their families across the street. The teacher who supervises them greets us with a grin, and says to Dylan, "That's quite a leaf, you've got there, little one!" Dylan grins back, affirms "Leaf!" and holds the leaf out to her. The teacher takes the leaf with solemn thanks and a warm smile. "Thank you, leaf baby," she says, and Dylan says, "Thank you," and we go on into the school.

And, so, a ritual is born.

Each morning, for three or four weeks, Dylan chooses a leaf to carry to her sister's school. Each morning, the teacher at the corner greets her: "Leaf baby! Look at the leaf you brought today! Thank you." Each morning, the leaf baby smiles back and offers her own thanks, and her own warm smile.

A leaf, specially chosen because of its—well, because of **what**? Its color? Its size? Its symmetry—or its a-symmetry? I don't know what Dylan's criteria were, but she was surely deliberate in her selection. A leaf, carried from home, generously offered to a person both familiar and not really known. A leaf, honoring place and relationship. With the ritual of that leafy morning gift, repeated for a stretch of days, Dylan's ecological identity (and perhaps that of the teacher) was confirmed and expanded.

A ritual is a gesture of hope and faith. Something happens that matters to us, that touches our hearts, stirs our spirits, engages our minds, and we memorialize that experience with a ritual. We re-enact it, in the hope that it will happen again. With ritual, we acknowledge that we have been fortunate and blessed, and we align ourselves with the possibility of further fortune, further blessing. Through ritual, we keep faith with what has mattered to us, and with ritual we position ourselves for another encounter with goodness, with gladness, with the reverberant generosity of life.

References

Laura Simms. *Our Secret Territory: The Essence of Storytelling.* Boulder, CO: Sentient Publications, 2011.

Webster's Seventh New Collegiate Dictionary. Springfield, MA: G. & C. Merriam, 1965.

A Call
to Come Home

We shall not cease from exploration
And the end of all our exploring
Will be to arrive where we started
And know the place for the first time.

T.S. Eliot, "Little Gidding"

Among my earliest memories are memories of place.

In the early winter dark, I walk on top of the snow plowed high at the sidewalk's edge. It is dense-packed, a winter's accumulation of snow compressed to form a ridgeline that I follow from one end of the block to the other and back again. The snow sparkles with the light of street lamps. The neighborhood is quiet, I am quiet, there is only the enveloping black sky and the shimmering white snow and the crunch of my feet and my soaring heart.

My brothers and I moisten the sand in the sandbox with bucketfuls of water carried from the spigot across the yard. Though we know nothing of the archipelago but its mythic character as a handful of tropical isles scattered like green jewels in a distant sea, my brothers and I have decided to carve the Hawaiian islands into the damp sand of our backyard. We wet the sand and shape it into a dozen mounding rises, some round, some long and thin, some crescent-curved. The afternoon is hot; I remember the sand's surface warmth and the pleasure of its cool under-layers. When the islands are shaped just as we want them, with channels carved deep around them, John and David and I fill our buckets again, and, with some ceremony and no small glee, we flood the channels with water.

Across from my childhood home is a small ravine that the kids in the neighborhood call 'the gully.' It is a dusty, dry, shallow trench edged by lodge pole pines; along its sandy bottom grows a sparse handful of plants, mostly wild grasses and brittle-branched bushes. The gully is forbidden territory; a young boy died there years earlier, suffocating when he was buried in the sandy slope where he'd been digging. My parents tell me the story of the dead boy at the start of each summer as a warning to stay out of the gully. But I don't stay out. I slide out of our yard, and cross the street, and tumble into the gully, an edge of fear rimming my desire to be in that wild place. It smells of pine and dust, the hot-summer scent of my childhood. I make my way along the sloping floor of the gully. The gully becomes the world, all-encompassing and compelling, and I am brave, and alone.

I knew my home ground intimately as a child—intimately, but unconsciously. "Water? What water?" asks the fish, in the teaching koan. The night sky and mounded snow along the suburban street, our backyard sandbox, sun and spigot water, the sharp-cut gully fragrant with dry-land summer—this wasn't 'nature,' it was simply home.

I grew up and left home and moved to new land, and that land was not home. It was beautiful and evocative, and I engaged it with muscle and gladness, but I lived there displaced from the feel of easy belonging to the land that I knew as a child. After two decades of displacement, I was ready to leave. I expected that my year with Dylan would be my last year in the Northwest, and thought of my time with Dylan as a prolonged goodbye to the green and damp.

It was, it turns out, a year-long homecoming.

The Northwest became home ground for me, because of my year with Dylan.

Or, more accurately, I came home to the Northwest. The land didn't change; I changed. My ecological identity became bound together with the place where I lived.

What changed in me?

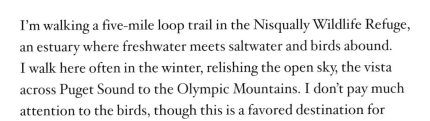

I'm walking a five-mile loop trail in the Nisqually Wildlife Refuge, an estuary where freshwater meets saltwater and birds abound. I walk here often in the winter, relishing the open sky, the vista across Puget Sound to the Olympic Mountains. I don't pay much attention to the birds, though this is a favored destination for devoted birders.

Today, though, is different.

A few days before this walk, Dylan and I stood at a bird feeder in a neighbor's yard and watched a tiny, round bird with lovely flashes of yellow on its brown-streaked wings. The bird charmed us with its quick movements, its occasional inversions to hang upside-down on the feeder, with the tilt of its head and the brightness of its eyes. When I got home that night, I did something I'd never done before. I looked up the bird on a birding website, because I wanted to know its name. It was a Pine Siskin.

Now, walking in the wildlife refuge, I watch for pine siskins. I don't see any. I do see a slate gray bird with a bold white face and belly, tiny as a siskin, dancing from branch to branch, upside-down, rightside-up, quick-moving. Who is this bird, I wonder. Is it some type of siskin? Are siskins and this bird part of a larger family of birds? My curiosity surprises me: it's not a passing or idle wondering, but a desire to know. I am suddenly tearful, which startles and irritates me. I am on a course for Utah, for Montana, for someplace not-here. I do not need to have my heart crack open to this place. This is not my place to love!

But that's what begins to happen, because of that gray and white bird. I want to know its name. I want to know who lives in this place with me, which means, I acknowledge ruefully and with no small release, that my residency here has begun.

I stop at the visitor center as I leave the refuge and buy a bird field guide. The bird I saw was a White-Breasted Nuthatch.

Siskin, nuthatch: birds as ordinary as sparrows and wrens. Not birder's prizes, nothing to record on a lifetime birding list. But these two tiny birds perched on my heart. And my heart welcomed them.

I didn't become a birder—that's not what changed in me.

What changed was my long acceptance of being displaced— my willingness to live on hold, gazing at the far horizon for home-somewhere-else, somewhere more suited to me than the gray, cool place where I lived. That day at the Nisqually Wildlife Refuge, I decided to shift my gaze from the horizon to the White-Breasted Nuthatch in front of me, and call it by its name. I decided to reside here, for as long as I lived here—which might not be forever. But while here, I wanted to be here fully. Walking the land, learning the names, filling my senses with this place. Making ritual, learning the stories, coming to know the goodness of rain. I decided to make this place home.

I did eventually move an hour away from Seattle, to a green river valley where I lived for several years in a cabin ringed by cedar, hemlock, and vine maple. I worked on a farm in the valley for a season, and wrote about it for the city folks who ate the food we grew. And then I left the river valley to return to the city, where the rain falls differently than in the valley, and where the sky is different, and the movement of creatures across the land and sky is different. But it is still the Northwest, and it is still my home, and I am easy in it.

Being outside, every day, with Dylan, inviting her to braid herself into this place, re-aligned me with this place. Nourishing Dylan's ecological identity re-enlivened my ecological identity. Inviting Dylan to know her home ground carried me home.

This is what I want for all of us, children and adults, wherever we live: an ecological identity, born in a particular place and grown from a sensual, emotional, and conscious connection to the land. An ecological identity that shapes us as surely as our cultural and social identities. An ecological identity that allows us to inhabit the Earth with awareness and honor. An ecological identity that grounds us in our home places and orients us to the world beyond our home places. An ecological identity that holds necessary intelligence as we confront the environmental calamity that is consuming the Earth.

"Life wants to live. Life so completely wants to live," writes Derrick Jensen. "And to the degree that we ourselves are alive, and to the degree that we consider ourselves among and allied with the living, our task is clear: to help life live." When we are grounded in an ecological identity, we are alive and allied with the living. When we are grounded in an ecological identity, we learn the names of birds, and we speak those names with the gladness of knowledge. And we speak *for* those birds, we act on their behalf. We live from a stance of what Kathleen Dean Moore calls 'applied reverence,' bearing joyful witness to the miracle of this planet and allying ourselves with it, to help life live.

References

T.S. Eliot, "Little Gidding" in *T. S. Eliot: Collected Poems, 1909-1962*. Orlando, FL: Harcourt, Brace, and Company, 1963.

Kathleen Dean Moore, in an interview in *High Country News*, September 14, 2009.

Derrick Jensen, "Side with the Living," in *Orion Magazine*, September-October 2009.

One Wild Spirit

Every blade of grass, every grasshopper,
every sparrow and twig
courses with a wild energy.
The same energy pours through me.
I rock slightly with the
slow pulse of my heart. . . .
My breath and the clouds ride the same wind.

Scott Russell Sanders, *A Conservationist Manifesto*

I kept a daily journal for Dylan during the year that she and I spent together. Each day, while Dylan napped, I wrote, recording how we'd spent the day, and what seemed especially resonant for Dylan, and what touched my heart. The stories in this book come from that journal.

It seems fitting to close my writing, in this book, with the writing that closed my year with Dylan.

September 15, 2009

Dear Dylan,

There is in you a seamlessness with the natural world.
You lean in and the world leans in and where you meet,
you melt together, so there is no solid line dividing you,
no demarcating border, but instead, a blurring of identities,
yours and the great wild world.

This is how I saw that seamlessness in you, this morning at
the beach:

We arrived at the beach at low tide. A heron stood in the tide flats,
its neck outstretched and head angled, gazing unblinkingly into
the shallow water. You stood at the water's edge, steady and still
and silent, watching the heron. I want to write that everything
beyond the beach and the heron faded away, but that's not
correct. It was more that everything stepped closer: the heron,
the saltwater, the sky, the mountains, the tide pool, the seagulls,
the breeze, the sun, you, me, all come together into an integrated
whole, a full and pulsing liveliness of attention and immediacy.

Breath and breeze and wave, heartbeat and heron, turning tide and watchful waiting—all expressions of one wild spirit.

After quite a stretch of time, a passing boat startled the heron into flight, and, squawking and complaining, the heron took off across the sky. You turned, then, to the tide pools.

Ankle deep in the sun-warmed shallows, you bent low over sea urchins, your cautious finger like a whisper on their round, supple bodies. You teased anemones, inciting their quick closure with a touch to their waving tentacles. You lifted rocks to scuttle tiny crabs out from their dark refuge. You stepped carefully around a large dead crab, still heavy with meat.

Eventually, you turned from the tide pool and settled onto the sandy beach. There, you piled cool, wet sand onto your legs, and sifted warm, dry sand onto your arms, and dipped a broken clam shell into a pool of saltwater and poured that water onto your belly. You dug your bare feet into the beach, hollowing a trough in the sand and watching the water rise into the hollow—and then you scooted your whole body into the new-made pool, laughing at its cool touch, laughing at the mud on your feet, laughing at the crow watching you laugh from a boulder just out of reach.

Oh, you were reluctant to leave the beach this morning, Dylan. "Goodbye, heron," you called as we made our way up the beach. "Goodbye, crab. Goodbye, mud. Goodbye, shell." And "goodbye" meant "love" and "yes" and "gratitude" and "us, here, together."